The Children of Mordecai

The Soper Journey in America

John Laycock

John Laycock

The Children of Mordecai

Print Version ISBN 979-8-218-16927-5
Ebook Version ISBN 979-8-218-16928-2

First Printing, 2023

CONTENTS

CONTENTS

Introduction

Mordecai Soper (1746-1824) and his descendants tread a path across a young nation starting in 1770 when Mordecai married Naomi Owen (1751-1836) in Connecticut. Along the way, there would be many stories of love, heartache, adventure, and most of all perseverance. There are soldiers (Revolutionary War, War of 1812, Civil War, and World War I), there are farmers, teamsters, millers, lawyers, doctors, gold miners, iron miners, loggers, explorers, inventors (with patents and their invention in the Smithsonian), Texas Supreme Court Justices, Jay-hawkers, prohibitionists, and murders.

The genesis of my interest in this history is from where I was born in Lake County, Illinois. Mordecai's grandchildren began showing up in Lake County during the 1840's. This writeup is in no way complete or finished. It is simply a starting point to gather some of these stories into one place and show a few generations of a family as they start in Connecticut and wind their way through Vermont, New York, Michigan, Ohio, Wisconsin, Illinois, Iowa, Kansas, Nebraska, Colorado, Nevada, Utah, Idaho, Oregon, California and as far west as China. It is also not intended to be an authoritative resource, but hopefully a framework for future research. It is based on a compilation of research from multiple sources. I've tried to be as thorough as possible. Any mistakes are mine and not intentional. I've tried to focus on having solid sources (avoiding family lore) to support my conclusions.

Tracking through multiple generations of families has proven to be a daunting task and much larger than I realized at the start of this project. By the numbers, Mordecai and Naomi had 10 children,

56 grandchildren and 162 great-grandchildren. There are 134 persons profiled herein, some more in depth than others. There will be missing information and regrettably unintended omissions. Systematically going through all of these families allows information and various relationships in different sources to emerge. It was not a trivial exercise but it has paid many dividends in my research.

John Laycock

February 2023

Acknowledgements

These acknowledgements will be by no means complete. Any errors and any omissions are not meant to be a slight and I apologize in advance.

While not related to researching the Soper family, I'd like to mention my cousin, Don Lewis. We met online many years ago while we were each researching the Laycock family lines. Don had done a tremendous amount of research on the Philadelphia based Laycocks and had been working on a tome to document them. A copy of which is now in the Cook Library in Libertyville, Illinois. Several years later that inspired me to start down this road and capture as much as I could about Mordecai and his descendants.

When I started doing genealogy I chased the Soper Compendium. I finally was able to locate a copy of the section on Mordecai. I found I kept seeing the names Dora Lampton Morse, Stanley Doran and Ray Elblein who were contributors to the Soper Compendium. Much of my research is based on climbing over their backs. I later had the privilege of talking with cousin Ray who still resides in Lake County. His quiet, unspoken efforts are reflected in a lot of this book.

As I entered the final stages of finishing this project, I re-connected with cousin Mary Grindol. We've been feverishly trading emails comparing notes and it has been a lot of fun. She was very helpful in sorting out the War of 1812 veterans. I first met Mary as I was getting started in genealogy. We had lost touch and I recently found her Ancestry account and was able to get back in touch.

Jim Ballard is the Milton, Vermont town historian. We've corresponded on several different Soper related topics. His wife, like Mary and Ray, is also a descendant of Mordecai.

Most importantly, I'd like to thank my wife, Elizabeth. Trust me when I say she has the patience of a saint. To my kids, Zachary, Addison, and Piper. I love you all more than you will ever know.

Research Notes

There are many ways to read through the information shared within. For each person described I have endeavored to include as much information as I possibly can in a somewhat structured format. I have also tried to include interesting details as I have found them. Each person presented here will have their name, date of birth, marriage and death as I know them. I will include where they lived during their lifetime, a list of children, and any sources regarding that individual.

Like many folks in the last 20 years, I started out by setting up a family tree on Ancestry. My skills have grown as I have learned about other research techniques, but at the end of the day it is a good home base.

Census data is a powerful place to start, particularly for families after 1850 when the census bureau began listing more than just the head of household. This has presented some blind spots in my research, particularly in my ancestral line through Mary Melissa Soper (1820-1852). She was born in 1820 and first appears in the 1850 census AFTER she was married to Charles Gray (1816-1886). I ended up taking a more roundabout path to connecting her to her parents Joseph Soper (1783-1851) and Electa Mansfield (1790-1865) through a combination of death certificates for her daughters, Angeline Charlotte Gray 1844-1925) and Mary Melissa Gray (1845-1933), an obituary for her daughter Angeline Charlotte Gray, an 1857 Minnesota State Census, and other supporting documentation.

When performing research in Lake County, Illinois there are some great contemporary accounts that be of use.

1. The Portrait and Biographical Album of Lake County, Illinois (1891)
2. The Past and Present of Lake County (1877)
3. Historical and Statistical Sketches of Lake County (1852)
4. History of Lake County (Halsey, 1912)

Note that the Portrait and Biographical Albums cover many counties in Illinois. What is great about some of these volumes is that not only are they in many cases, contemporary accounts, but they are also out of print books which can be found online fairly easily. Many times when I come across a research citation like this for an older research volume I will do a search for it on Google Books, Open Library or archive.org. If the repository has the book, it will often be easily available in a pdf format that can be downloaded for further offline research. CTRL-F is your friend.

The Lake County Vital Records website has a searchable index for older records that is very useful. (https://www.lakecountyil.gov/398/Genealogical-Records-Search) Index records can be searched and a request for genealogical copies at a very reasonable rate can be made by mail. This was particularly useful looking up marriage records as the Sopers began arriving in Lake County.

Another great Lake County resource are the research librarians (thank you Jen Barry and Sonia Schoenfield) at the Cook Library in Libertyville. They have been amazingly helpful in steering me in different directions. Through the course of this research, I've been able to help add information to my Rogers and Laycock family files in their collection. I hope to add this volume to their collection as well.

One last Illinois resource is the Civil War soldier database lookup, which is located here: https://apps.ilsos.gov/isaveterans/civilMusterSearch.do This was very helpful to identify the units the Conklin family members served under and their service dates. Clarissa Soper (1811-1882) like so many mothers had a husband, three sons, a stepson, and son-in-law fight for the Grand Army of the Republic.

The Michigan research I did was greatly aided by the Michigan Pioneer and Historical Society Collections Volume 31 (1901). This was also supplemented by the invaluable Bureau of Land Management General Land Records database, https://glorecords.blm.gov/search. Many family members that moved to Benzie County were able to homestead there. This database is also useful for looking up land bounty records from Revolutionary and War of 1812 veterans.

For general reference the following are various land grants created by the US Government to encourage westward expansion:

Land Act of 1820 - https://en.wikipedia.org/wiki/Land_Act_of_1820

Preemption Act of 1841 - https://en.wikipedia.org/wiki/Preemption_Act_of_1841

Donation Land Claim Act of 1850 - https://en.wikipedia.org/wiki/Donation_Land_Claim_Act

Land Grant Act of 1850 - https://en.wikipedia.org/wiki/Land_Grant_Act_of_1850

1862 Homestead Act - https://en.wikipedia.org/wiki/Homestead_Acts

In addition to the more general land grant programs, there were land bounty programs for War of 1812 and Revolutionary War veterans. There were acts in 1842, 1850, 1852, and 1855 that allowed the land to be sold or given to descendants. There are files with the National Archives that can contain more information on the application process. They can be a useful source of additional information. It was useful uncovering a great deal of additional information about Electa Soper (1790-1865) and her trials applying for the land bounty for her husband Joseph Soper (1783-1851). After the death of Joseph we can see her moving west with her children and stopping to make various court filings certifying her eligibility for the land grant. There are written affidavits attesting to her marriage to Joseph in 1807 and naming some of their children.

War of 1812 pension records and land bounty records can be obtained directly from the National Archives (https://www.archives.gov/research/military/army/pensions) and in some cases are available through the Fold3 website. I would recommend checking both to see what you get back. As an example of why you should check both, the National Archives had a file on Joseph Soper, but Fold3 did not.

The Bureau of Land Management General Land Records database is endlessly fascinating and can be used to track the homesteading land grants and the land bounty applications. https://glorecords.blm.gov/search/default.aspx

Vermont in particular deserves a shoutout for their Vital Records database. Many of the Milton, Vermont relatives had birth, marriage, and death records available through that database which I accessed through the Ancestry website.

Newspapers.com has been a more recent addition to my toolbox and is readily useful for finding death notices, obituaries and various news articles. I made extensive use of it when looking over the Julia Jane Soper (1830-1884) murder and the William Pierson (1871-1935) and Lena Haskell (1877-1935) murders. More on the Pierson murders can be found on the podcast, Tenfold More Wicked: Murder in the Court from 2021. https://www.tenfoldmorewicked.com/

Additional newspapers not in newspapers.com from Vermont can be found online at the University of Vermont Library at http://library.uvm.edu/vtnp/?tag=lamoille-newsdealer and through the Library of Congress at https://chroniclingamerica.loc.gov/newspapers/?state=Vermontðnicity=&language=.

Another fairly new resource for me has a number of newspapers list for New York state:

https://nyshistoricnewspapers.org. I have not made extensive use of this, but New York state has been a bit of a blind spot for my research efforts so I am looking forward to digging into this resource.

Two good resources for historical accounts in Milton and Chittenden County can be found in the following two publications which are available online at archive.org and can be downloaded in a pdf format:

1. Gazetteer and business directory of Chittenden County, Vermont, for 1882-83.
   Syracuse, N.Y., Printed at the Journal Office. 1882.
2. History of Chittenden County, Vermont. Syracuse, N.Y. : D. Mason & Co.1886.

Some key information about John Bean (1781-1872) and others was found in the Gazetteer and business directory of Chittenden County, Vermont publication.

The telling of the Haskell's in Nebraska was aided incredibly by the book, "The Trail of the Loup; being a history of the Loup River region" by Foght, Harold Waldstein, 1906.

https://archive.org/details/trailofloupbeing00fogh

This book was written by Harold Foght (1870-1954) who was married to Alice Mabel Robbins (1878-1952), a grand-daughter of Harriet Eveline Soper (1823-1890). The book tells the history of Ord, Nebraska.

Staying with the Haskell family for a moment, Irma Imogene Haskell (1891-1968) was living in China when she returned to Nevada to marry John William "J.W." Dunfee (1875-1931). In 1927 J.W. struck gold in Hornsilver, Nevada, later renamed Gold Point, Nevada. More on the Dunfee's can be learned from the 2007 book by Alan Patera, "Hornsilver / Gold Point Nevada Silver turns to Gold".

Some key resources for the Sopers in Iowa include the following:

"History of Buchanan County, Iowa". Cleveland, Williams brothers. 1881 https://archive.org/details/historyofbuchana00will/page/306/mode/2up

"History of Franklin and Cerro Gordo counties, Iowa" 1883. https://archive.org/details/historyoffrankli01unio

"Iowa : its history and its foremost citizens" 1918. Chicago : S. J. Clarke. Retrieved from

https://archive.org/details/iowaitshistoryit01brig

There is also a website dedicated to the history of Maysville, Iowa. It has pictures and transcribed newspaper obituaries see http://www.maysvilleiowa.com.

There is a fascinating series of letters posted on the Ancestry website, called "A Simple Story of Life and Love on the Dakota Plains" compiled by John Manning Stewart in 2006. It contains a series of letters from Helen Thurnau (1875-1960) to Phoebe Laura Kennedy (1892–1940) written in the 1930's. Phebe was Orange Phelps Soper's (1828-1888) granddaughter through his daughter, Laura Idella Soper (1872-1893). Note, this is Remember Soper's (1794-1872) son. Phoebe and her brother, Harold Malcolm Kennedy (1893-1931) were agonizingly put up for adoption by her father, John Henry Kennedy (1863-1919) after her mother, Laura died at a young age. John never got over it and later remarried to Helen Thurnau who shared the circumstances behind her adoption and how deeply it affected her birth father.

Mordecai Soper (1746-1824)

Mordecai Soper (1746-1824) is believed to have been born in Windsor, Connecticut, though some accounts state he was born in England. Mordecai married Naomi Owen (1751-1836) in Litchfield, Connecticut on April 4, 1770.

Naomi was born in Connecticut on March 3, 1751, and her parents were Elijah Woodworth Owen (1720-1799) and Patience Wright (1729-1756). Elijah's family is Welsh and dates back to the 1600's in Connecticut. Patience's family is English and dates back to Massachusetts in the 1600's. Naomi's older sister, Sarah Owen, (1748-1787) married Heber Allen, a brother of Ethan and Ira Allen, both members of the Green Mountain Boys.

They had ten children together. Their oldest children, Elizabeth Soper (1770-1846) and Elijah Soper (1773-1792), were born in Connecticut. The Sopers would be on the move and in 1775 William Soper (1775-1792) was born in Poultney, Vermont.

While they were in Poultney, during 1780-1781, Mordecai served as a private in the Vermont militia. Mordecai is listed on the payroll of Captain Zebediah Dewey's Company for service done in October 1780. He is also listed on the payroll of Captain Abisha Moseley's Company supporting the Alarm at Castleton on June 10, 1781 and again October 21, 1781. During this time, as described in the Abby Hemingway Vermont Historical Gazetteer, some families were sent back to Connecticut for safety which may be why Ruth Soper (1778-?) was born in Connecticut. Joseph Soper (1783-1851) and Erastus Soper (1785-1857) were subsequently born in Poultney, Vermont.

Mordecai and Naomi's growing family moved to Milton in 1787 where Mordecai took the Freeman's Oath on May 3, 1787. The town was first settled by William Irish, Leonard Owen, Amos Mansfield, Absalom Taylor, and Thomas Dewey. Mordecai's son, Joseph, married Amos Mansfield's daughter Electa. The Sopers were one of the early founding families of Milton and by 1795 there were approximately 300 settlers living in Milton. Mordecai and Naomi's children, Charity Soper (1789-1847), Electa Lake Soper (1792-1869), Remember Elijah Soper (1794-1872), and Phebe Soper (1795-1867) were all born in Milton.

Based on an account in the Vermont Gazette, on December 7, 1792, sons Elijah and William died in a canoeing accident. The Gazette states that two boys by the name of Soper, one by the name of Owen and another by Irish are believed to have perished. There are no further records of Elijah and William after this date. The Owen boy may be their uncle, Ambrose Owen (1770-1792) whose name is found in a Town of Milton death record from November 20, 1792. Later in 1794 Mordecai and Naomi would welcome another son, named Remember Elijah (1794-1872), likely a nod to honor his older brother Elijah.

Mordecai died on August 6, 1821 and is buried in Milton Plains Cemetery. Some sources claim he died in 1824 but based on his gravestone and his Town of Milton death record, both indicate he died in 1821. Naomi died on April 10, 1836 in Milton, Vermont and is buried in Miltonboro Cemetery.

Migration:
1746 Connecticut
1770 Connecticut
1775 Poultney, Vermont
1787 Milton, Vermont
1821 Milton, Vermont

Children:
Elizabeth Soper (1770-1846)

Elijah Soper (1773-1792)

William Soper (1775-1792)

Ruth Soper (1778-?)

Joseph Soper (1783-1851)

Erastus Soper (1785-1857)

Charity Soper (1789-1847)

Electa Lake Soper (1792-1869)

Remember Elijah Soper (1794-1872)

Phebe Soper (1795-1867)

Sources:

1790 Census

1800 Census

1810 Census

1821 Vermont Vital Record - Town of Milton, Death Record

1821 Find A Grave

The State of Vermont. Rolls of the Soldiers in the Revolutionary War 1775 to 1783. Rutland, Vermont, USA: Tuttle, 1904.Original data: Goodrich, John E. pg 382, 513

The Barbour Collection of Connecticut Town Vital Records. Vol 37 pg 103, Marriage Record

Portrait and Biographical Album of Lake County, Illinois 1891. Pg 643-644

Elizabeth Soper (1770-1846)

Elizabeth Soper (1770-1846)

Elizabeth Soper (1770-1846) was born in Salibury, Connecticut on October 16, 1770, and moved around with her family, eventually settling in Milton, Vermont. A Town of Milton birth record indicates she had an illegitimate son named Orange Phelps on March 1, 1793. In the 1820 census she was living in Milton and listed as head of the household. Elizabeth passed away in Milton on May 20, 1846. She is buried in Miltonboro Cemetery in a shared marker with her son Orange Phelps and his family. Her death record does not indicate she was married.

Migration:
1770 Connecticut
1775 Poultney, Vermont
1787 Milton, Vermont
1846 Milton, Vermont

Children:
Orange Phelps (1793-1885)

Sources:
1770 The Barbour Collection of Connecticut Town Vital Records. Vol 37 pg 103, Birth Record
1793 Vermont Vital Record - Town of Milton, Birth Record
1820 Census
1846 Vermont Vital Record - Town of Milton, Death Record

1846 Find A Grave

Orange Phelps (1793-1885)

Orange was born on March 1, 1893 to Elizabeth Soper in Milton, Vermont. His birth record lists him as an illegitimate child and there is no father listed. In his youth, he served in the War of 1812 in Captain Amasa Mansfield's company under Colonel Luther Dixon's Regiment with his uncles, Joseph, Erastus and Remember Soper and Isaiah Martin. Orange notably fought in the Battle of Plattsburgh in September 1814, a battle which effectively ended the British invasion of the northern United States.

Through his life Orange rose far above the what must have been scandalous circumstances of his birth. His front page death notice from the Argus and Patriot newspaper on December 2, 1885 painted a picture of how respected and well regarded he was. Orange had two of the three uncles he served with in the War of 1812, name their children "Orange Phelps" Soper after him.

As attested in his War of 1812 pension application (see his War of 1812 Declaration of Soldier for Pension from March 17, 1871) Orange married Sarah Miner (1796-1873) on June 16, 1818. He is listed in the 1820, 1830, and 1850 census and lived in Milton, Vermont. His War of 1812 pension files from the National Archives show that on January 15, 1851 Orange appeared in Chittenden County Court before Justice of the Peace, Daniel Squires. He filed to grant power of attorney to A.L. Gage, a Washington DC based attorney, to pursue a bounty land warrant for his service in Captain Amasa Mansafield's Company in the War of 1812.

Included in Orange's pension application are two testimonies provided from Isaiah Martin (1781-1859) and Henry McLaughlin. Henry McLaughlin appeared before the Justice of the Peace in Chittenden County on February 6, 1851 and stated he was in the army in 1813 for about three months and was acquainted with Orange Phelps during that time.

Isaiah Martin appeared before the Justice of the Peace in Chittenden County on August 4, 1851 to attest that he served with Orange Phelps for about two months in Captain Amasa Mansfield's Company starting in September 1813. This is notable for the pension application of Amasa Mansfield (1792-1875) shows a claim made by Amasa was that he served in Captain Amasa Mansfield's Company as a substitute for Isaiah Martin. Though records listed Isaiah serving during that time as a sergeant Captain Amasa Mansfield's Company.

In 1854 Orange received a Bounty Land Claim under the September 28, 1850: ScripWarrant Act of 1850 (9 Stat. 520) for his War of 1812 service. Records provided from the United States Department of the Interior Bureau of Land Management General Land Office Records indicate he served as a private in Captain Mansfield's company in the Vermont Militia in the War of 1812. He was granted 40 acres in Rock Island County, Illinois on October 2, 1854 under Military Warrant Volume 824 pg 390, Document #54029. The land was sold to William W. White for an undisclosed sum.

His War of 1812 pension files from the National Archives show that on April 11, 1855 he filed a second land bounty claim in Franklin County, Vermont, to grant permission to a new attorney, Charles W. Stilphen of Swanton, Vermont to prosecute his Land Bounty claim and procure his warrant under the March 3, 1855: ScripWarrant Act of 1855.

In 1860 Orange received the remaining 120 acres of his Bounty Land Claim this time under the March 3, 1855: ScripWarrant Act of 1855 (10 Stat. 701) for his War of 1812 service. Records provided from the United States Department of the Interior Bureau of Land Management General Land Office Records indicate he served as a private in Captain Mansfield's company in the Vermont Militia in the War of 1812. He was granted 120 acres in Buffalo County, Wisconsin on August 3, 1860 under Military Warrant Volume 174 pg 210, Document #55563. The land was sold to Alfred Street for an undisclosed sum.

Orange applied for a War of 1812 pension in 1871. The records are kept in the National Archives and have been retrieved through the Fold3 website. Orange appeared in Franklin County to file his War of 1812 Declaration of Soldier for Pension on March 17, 1871. He stated that he was 78 years old and married Sarah Minor on June 16, 1818 in Milton, Vermont. He attested that he was drafted into Captain Mansfield's Company at Milton, Vermont on the first day of September 1813 and was honorably discharged at Plattsburgh on or about the 12th day of September 1814. He referred to his Bounty Land Warrant for proof of service. The Declaration was signed by Orange and his attorney A.G. Brush. It was witnessed by his son Heman A. Phelps and Judson A. Carr. Judson was the brother of two of Orange's daughter in laws, Julia Carr (1823-1904) and Jane Carr (1828-1907). An official stamp shows the Declaration was received by the Department of the Interior Pension Office on May 29, 1871.

The application was assigned Certificate #16518. In the Brief of Claim for a Survivor's Pension form from the Pension Office, Orange Phelps was credited by the Third Auditors Group in the United States Treasury Department with serving 54 days in Captain Amsa Mansfield's Company September 25, 1813 through November 17, 1813. The claim was rejected on June 3, 1872 for insufficient days of service; he needed 60 days to receive the pension of $8/month.

Orange reapplied for the pension in early 1873. The application was assigned a new Certificate #20312. In the Brief of Claim for a Survivor's Pension form from the Pension Office, Orange Phelps was credited by the Third Auditors Group in the United States Treasury Department with serving 54 days in Captain Amsa Mansfield's Company September 25, 1813 through November 17, 1813. They referenced his Bounty Land application. In addition to the Third Auditor's report, the Pension Office accepted the affidavit from R.E. Soper that Orange served with him in Captain Beeman's Company at the Battle of Plattsburgh from September 6 through 13, 1814. This gave Orange a total of 62 days in service and qualified him for the pension benefit of $8/month.

This was admitted on January 28, 1873. The document was readmitted on February 11, 1873 once R.E. Soper's statement was notarized by a clerk of the court.

Remember Elijah Soper (1794-1872) appeared in Franklin County court on November 9, 1872 to testify that Orange served with him in Captain Beeman's Company in September of 1814. He died shortly after that on November 24, 1872. This statement was signed by Remember on November 9, 1872 and the Pension Office received the document on December 27, 1872. Among the documents there is a handwritten note asking if Orange's attorney HA Brush is a notary. The statement was sent back to Brush asking him on January 30, 1872 to have the character statement from Remember notarized by a clerk of the court. This was done on February 4, 1872 and the paperwork was officially received and completed by the Pension Office on February 10, 1872.

Given the death of Remember, Brush must have asked Orange for another character witness. On December 16, 1872 Amasa Mansfield appeared in court in Traverse City to attest that he served with Orange in Captain Beeman's Company. This document was filed in court and witnessed by Amasa's daughter Maria Lake (1833-1897) and Thomas Cook. Orange's lawyer HA Brush submitted this to the Pension Office in a letter dated December 23, 1872 which was received by the Pension Office on December 27, 1872. .

There are two distinct mentions of Orange Phelps mining iron ore in the Milton area. The first is from January 1829 and is mentioned in the Vermont Chronicle, The Repertory, and the Journal of the Times in similar forms. They state a bed of iron ore was discovered in West Milton near the lake shore and that the owner was Orange Phelps.

This matches an entry in the United States Geological Survey (USGS) Mineral Resource Data System (MRDS) database for "Orange Phelps Iron Mine" (Deposit ID #10089820 MRDS ID #W033677). This location is east of Lake Rd, near Misty Bay Rd at 44°42'29.9"N 73°12'13.4"W.

In late November 1872, there were articles in the the Burlington Free Press and the Argus and Patriot sharing that Orange Phelps, Isaiah Martin, HA Phelps, George Phelps and Z.D. Everest had deeded the right to dig on their farms for iron or other ores to to A.H. Brainard of Oneida County. They were paid at a rate of $25 per acre that Brainard occupied. HA and George Phelps are Orange's sons. Orange served in the War of 1812 with Isaiah Martin's (1820-1885) father who was also named Isaiah Martin (1781-1859) but had passed away previously. Isaiah, George and HA are all cousins through Isaiah's mother, Charity Soper (1789-1847) and Orange's mother Elizabeth Soper (1770-1846) who were sisters.

Looking through the MRDS database, there are two other possible mine locations belonging to Orange. The first is named the "Phelps Iron Mine" (Deposit ID #10081574 MRDS ID #W033685). This location is east of River Road and south of Bergeron Rd at 44°56'41.9"N 72°23'20.0"W.

The second is named the "Orange Phelps Mine" (Deposit ID # 10084665 MRDS ID #W102087) This location is near Lake Carmi off Vermont Route 108, south of Stanley Hill Rd at 44°58'24.9"N 72°49'28.2"W.

In the 1860 census he was living in Bombay, New York. In early 1870 Orange returned to Vermont and bought the Ezekial Hildreth farm in West Corinth, Vermont. Sarah died in Corinth in 1873. In 1880 Orange was back in Milton, Vermont with his son, George. Orange died on November 23, 1885, and is buried in Miltonboro Cemetery along with his wife Sarah, his mother Elizabeth and his sons, Orange and Stephen.

It is worth noting that there are two Orange Phelps living in the Milton area during the early to mid 1800's. The Orange Phelps (1793-1885) discussed here lived most of his life in Milton, until the 1860's when he moved for a time to Bombay, New York. He eventually returned home to Milton for his final years in early 1870.

The other Orange Phelps (1806-1879) was a notable citizen being active in local politics by serving in the state legislature and as a judge through his life. He was born in nearby South Hero, Vermont to Bene-jah Phelps (1770-1862) and Elizabeth Graham (1776-1808). Orange Phelps (1806-1879) married a woman named Maria Phelps (1813-1882) in 1834. Maria's name is listed on the marriage record as Phelps, but that has not been researched further to verify its accuracy. Orange Phelps (1806-1879) also served on the board of the Vermont Mutual Insurance Company, representing Grand Isle County.

A simple way to sort out which Orange is which, is to look for the mention of South Hero or Grand Isle County in the record and that indicates it is likely the younger Orange Phelps (1806-1879).

Migration:
1793 Milton, Vermont
1860 Bombay, New York
1870 Corinth, Vermont
1880 Milton, Vermont
1885 Milton, Vermont

Children:
Orange Phelps (1819–1827)
Noah Phelps (1821–1860)
Julia Phelps (1823–1910)
Heman A. Phelps (1824–1901)
Stephen Phelps (1826–1827)
Charles Phelps (1827–1903)
Sarah M. Phelps (1829–1909)
George Willis Phelps (1831–1897)
Jane Phelps (1833–1866)
Delila Phelps (1835–1894)
Eveline M. Phelps (1838–1915)

Sources:

1793 Vermont, U.S., Vital Records, 1720-1908 - Town of Milton, Birth Record

1820 census

1830 census

1850 census

1860 census

1870 Purchase - Argus and Patriot - 3 Feb 1870 - Page 3

1870 census

1880 census

1885 Vermont, U.S., Vital Records, 1720-1908 - Town of Milton, Death Record

1885 Find a Grave

1885 Phelps Death Notice - Argus and Patriot. Montpelier, Vermont. December 02, 1885. Page 1

1885 Vermont, U.S., Wills and Probate Records, 1749-1999

War of 1812 records:

U.S., War of 1812 Pension Application Files Index, 1812-1815

List of War of 1812 soldiers - The Brandon Union. Brandon, Vermont. 12 Jul 1873, Sat. Page 2.

1933 Johnson, Herbert T. State of Vermont Roster of Soldiers in the War of 1812-1814. The Messenger Press. Pg 333.

Military Bounty Land Warrant Vol 174 pg 210. Document #55563. (120 Acres). August 31, 1860.

Military Bounty Land Warrant Vol 824 pg 390. Document #54029. (40 Acres) October 2, 1854.

Retrieved from https://glorecords.blm.gov/search/default.aspx

Mine Records:

Orange Phelps Iron Mine - https://mrdata.usgs.gov/mrds/show-mrds.php?dep_id=10089820

Possible Orange Phelps Iron Mine location - 44°56'41.9"N 72°23'20.0"W

Phelps Iron Mine - https://mrdata.usgs.gov/mrds/show-mrds.php?dep_id=10081574

Possible Phelps Iron Mine location - 44°56'41.9"N 72°23'20.0"W

Orange Phelps Mine - https://mrdata.usgs.gov/mrds/show-mrds.php?dep_id=10084665

Possible Orange Phelps Mine location - 44°42'29.9"N 73°12'13.4"W

The Repertory St. Albans, Vermont. 08 Jan 1829, Thu. Page 3.

Journal of the Times. Bennington, Vermont, 16 Jan 1829, Fri. Page 2.

Vermont Chronicle. Bellows Falls, Vermont. 23 Jan 1829, Fri. Page 3.

The Burlington Free Press. Burlington, Vermont. 26 Nov 1872, Tue. Page 3.

Argus and Patriot. Montpelier, Vermont. 28 Nov 1872, Thu. Page 3.

Burlington Weekly Free Press. 29 Nov 1872, Fri. Page 3.

Elijah Soper (1773-1792) and William Soper (1775-1792)

Elijah Soper (1773-1792) and William Soper (1775-1792)

From the Vermont Gazette, December 7, 1792, Elijah Soper (1773-1792) and William Soper (1775-1792) are believed to have drowned in a canoe accident at the age of 19 and 17 respectively. The Gazette states that two boys by the name of Soper, one by the name of Owen and another by Irish are believed to have perished. There are no further records of Elijah and William after this date. The Owen boy may be their uncle and Naomi's half-brother, Ambrose Owen (1770-1792); his name was found in a Town of Milton death record from November 20, 1792. In 1794 Mordecai and Naomi would welcome another son, named Remember Elijah (1794-1872), likely a nod to honor his older brother Elijah.

Migration:
1773 Connecticut
1775 Poultney, Vermont
1787 Milton, Vermont
1792 Milton, Vermont

Sources:
1773 The Barbour Collection of Connecticut Town Vital Records. Vol 37 pg 103, Birth Record
The Vermont Gazette - 7 Dec 1792 - Page 3

"Tombstone Tuesday: Remember Elijah Soper" - https://digging-history.com/2015/01/27/tombstone-tuesday-remember-elijah-soper/ retrieved 1 Jan 2022.

Ruth Soper (1778-?)

Ruth Soper (1778-?)

Ruth was born on August 16, 1778 in Salisbury, Connecticut. Ruth may have died before the move to Milton. One publication suggests she died in Connecticut a year after her birth but no records could be found.

Sources:

1778 The Barbour Collection of Connecticut Town Vital Records. Vol 37 pg 103, Birth Record

Joseph Soper (1783-1851)

Joseph Soper (1783-1851)

Joseph Soper (1783-1851) was born on July 7, 1851, in Poultney, Vermont and his wife, Electa Lake Mansfield (1790-1865), was born in Milton, Vermont. They married on July 9, 1807 in a ceremony performed by Stephen Mears. Joseph served in the War of 1812 as a private in the Vermont Volunteers Regiment of Rifleman. He served in Captain Amasa Mansfield's (an uncle to his wife Electa) company under Colonel Luther Dixon's Regiment, with his brothers Remember (1794-1872) and Erastus (1785-1857) Soper, nephew, Orange Phelps (1792-1885), and brother in law Isaiah Martin (1781-1859). By 1820 they moved from Milton, Vermont to Franklin County, New York and eventually to Lawrence, New York where Joseph drowned in the St. Lawrence River in January 1851. Joseph and Electa had 12 children together.

Bounty-land warrants for service in the War of 1812 gave surviving veterans land bounty under congressional acts of 1842, 1850, 1852, and 1855. Joseph initially applied for a land bounty from the US Government based on his service in the War of 1812 in 1850. After his passing in January 1851, Electa would take on the cause and several filings and written affidavits can be found in the National Archive records for Joseph's War of 1812 service. These affidavits are from several family and friends. Electa's mark can be seen in some of these records indicating she is not able to read or write.

After Joseph's death Electa begins moving west with her children. In October 1852 she filed paperwork in Lake County, Illinois stating she was a resident of Cook County. Her sworn testimony was affirmed by her brother-in-law Remember Soper and her son-in-law Edward Jones. Later in June 1853, Remember Soper and Reverend Salmon Stebbins affirmed Joseph and Electa were married and no records of the marriage to their knowledge existed.

By 1856, she was listed in the Iowa census as living with her son Orange Phelps Soper and his family in Alton, Iowa. Later that year in November Electa appeared before the court in Crawford County, Wisconsin. She stated she was a resident of Buchanan County, Iowa. She affirmed she was the widow of Joseph Soper who served under Captain Amasa Mansfield in the War of 1812. She further stated that she was married to Joseph on July 9, 1807 by Justice of the Peace Stephen Mears and her maiden name was Electa Mansfield. She also stated that her husband died on January 24, 1851. She declared that she was entitled to bounty land under the March 3, 1855: Scrip Warrant Act of 1855.

Electa had attempted to apply 4 years prior under A.S. Waterman of Waukegan, Illinois. This time, she appointed J.T. Neely of Washington DC, her attorney. This claim was witnessed by Abijah (1803-1867) and James Mansfield (1837-1905) of Alamakee County. Abijah is Amasa Mansfield's (1792-1875) brother. Amasa married Joseph's younger sister, Electa Soper. Alamakee County, Iowa and Crawford County, Wisconsin are located across the Mississippi River from each other. James is likely Abijah's son. Both Abijah's father, James Mansfield (1767-1849) and his brother James (1795-1855) are deceased at this point, and his brother James was still in New York.

Electa Soper (1792-1869) is the daughter of Mordecai Soper and Naomi Owen, Joseph's sister. She married Amasa Mansfield (1792-1875). He served as a private under his Uncle, Captain Amasa Mansfield's (1769-1847) company in Colonel Luther Dixon's Regiment with his future brother in laws, Joseph, Erastus and Remember Soper and Orange Phelps.

Joseph married Electa Lake Mansfield (1790-1865). Electa is the daughter of Amos Mansfield (1741-1795) and Mary Jackson (1748-1795). Many records confuse the matter, but in summary,

Mordecai and Naomi Soper's daughter, Electa Soper (1792-1869), married Amasa Mansfield (1792-1875) and became Electa Mansfield. Amos and Mary Mansfield's daughter, Electa Lake Mansfield (1790-1865), married Joseph Soper (1783-1851) and became Electa Soper.

In October 1858 Electa appointed yet another lawyer, L.F. Bingham of Chicago, Illinois, as her true and lawful attorney. She granted him power of attorney to obtain any Land Warrant on her behalf. Military Bounty Land Warrant records on the Bureau of Land Management website show that Electa was eventually awarded 160 acres in Sarpy County, Nebraska on October 1, 1860 under the March 3, 1855 Scrip Warrant Act of 1855 (10 Stat. 701). Her lawyer, L.F. Bingham signed the long sought after land bounty over to Darwin H Ranney for an undisclosed sum of money.

Electa lived a rather remarkable life. The daughter of a Revolutionary War veteran, she married Joseph Soper, the son of an Revolutionary War veteran in 1807 at the age of 16. While raising her family of 12 children she saw Joseph serve in the War of 1812. They moved from Milton, Vermont; Bombay, New York; Fort Covington, New York; Brasher Falls, New York; and eventually Lawrence, New York where Joseph tragically drowned in the St. Lawrence River. Following her children west after the death of her husband in 1851, we can see her make multiple court filings as she fought to receive his land bounty for serving in the War of 1812 which after ten years she finally received it in 1860 under the Scrip Warrant Act of 1855.

She followed her children to the prairies of the West, eventually crossing the Mississippi into Iowa, where she passed away on December 4, 1865 as the Civil War ended. She is buried in Fairbank Cemetery in Fairbank, Iowa while Joseph is buried over a thousand miles away in Haleville Cemetery in St. Lawrence County, New York.

Migration:
1783 Poultney, Vermont
1787 Milton, Vermont

1823 Bombay, New York
1830 Fort Covington, New York
1840 Brasher Falls, New York
1850 Lawrence, New York
1851 Lawrence, New York
(Electa)
1852 Lake County, Illinois
1856 Buchanan County, Iowa

Children:
William H. Soper (1809-1867)
Phoebe Soper (1810-?)
Clarissa Soper (1811-1882)
Naomi Lovina Soper (1813-1884)
Joseph Miles Soper (1815-1891)
Isaiah Martin Soper (1817-1861)
Mary Melissa Soper (1820-1852)
Harriet Eveline Soper (1823-1890)
Orange Phelps Soper (1827-1893)
Elizabeth Charity Soper (1829-1904)
James P. Soper (1831-1872)
Sarah Louisa Soper (1832-1909)

Sources:
1790 Census
1810 Census
1820 Census
1830 Census
1840 Census
1850 Census
Census Non-Population Schedules, 1850
1851 Find A Grave
War of 1812 Land Bounty Records (NARA)

Portrait and Biographical Album of Lake County, Illinois 1891. Page 643-644

1881 Iowa, Marriage Records, 1880-1937, Iowa State Archives; Des Moines, Iowa; Volume: 302 (Dubuque - Henry)

History of Chittenden County, Vermont. Syracuse, N.Y. : D. Mason & Co.1886.

Military Bounty Land Warrant Vol 380 pg 207. Retrieved from https://glorecords.blm.gov/search/default.aspx

Land Grant Act of 1850 https://en.wikipedia.org/wiki/ Land_Grant_Act_of_1850

Scrip Warrant Act of 1855

1933 Johnson, Herbert T. State of Vermont Roster of Soldiers in the War of 1812-1814. The Messenger Press. Pg 395-396

William H. Soper (1809-1867)

William H. Soper (1809-1867) was born in 1807 in Vermont and married Percy Reynolds (1814-1881). They had 10 children and lived in St Lawrence County, New York until at least 1850, The New York State Census in 1855 lists them as living in Pomfret, New York. By the 1860 census they are listed living in Reading, Michigan where William passed away on January 14, 1867, and is buried in Oak Grove Cemetery in Coldwater, Michigan. The 1870 Census shows Percy living with her son, William Henry Soper (1843-1923) in Quincy, Michigan. She passed away in 1881 and is also buried in Oak Grove Cemetery in Coldwater, Michigan. .

Migration:
1809 Milton, Vermont
1823 Bombay, New York
1830 Fort Covington, New York
1840 Brasher Falls, New York
1850 Louisville, New York
1860 Reading, MI

1867 Reading, MI

Children:
John M Soper (1834–1915)
Jeremiah Soper (1837–)
Electa Soper (1838–)
Naomi Lavina Soper (1840–1914)
Mary Melissa Soper (1841–1912)
William Henry Soper (1843–1923)
Oliver C Soper (1845–)
Rosette Chloe Soper (1847–1924)
James Joseph Soper (1850–1913)
Phebe E Soper (1852–1932)

Sources:
1840 Census
1850 Census
1855 NY State Census
1860 Census
1867 Find A Grave

John M Soper (1834–1915)

John M Soper (1834–1915) was born on May 15, 1833 in New York. He was married 3 times. His first wife was Sarah Ann Garrett (?-1868) and with her he had two children, William Soper (1867-1907) and Wealthy "Etta" Soper (1868-1931). His second wife was Melinda Van Slyke (1838-?) they were married on October 2, 1869. There is a Sylvia Jane "Jennie" Soper (1862-1945) listed as their daughter but records show she was born in 1862. Sylvia's death certificate does not list a mother. John married Louana Elizabeth Bundy in 1871 and they had 2 children, Carrie E. Soper (1871-1949) and Josephine N (1878-1946).

He died in Battle Creek, Michigan on March 5, 1915 and is buried in Coldwater, Michigan.

Migration:
1834 Fort Covington, New York
1840 Brasher Falls, New York
1850 Louisville, New York
1863 Reading, MI
1900 Coldwater, Michigan
1914 Battle Creek Michigan

Children:
With Sarah Ann Garrett:
William Soper (1867–1907)
Wealthy W "Etta" Soper (1868–1931)
With Louana Elizebeth Bundy (1850–)
Carrie E. Soper (1871–1949)
Josephine N. Soper (1878–1946)

Sources:
1850 Census
1855 NY State Census
1860 Census
U.S., Civil War Draft Registrations Records, 1863-1865
1869 Michigan, U.S., Marriage Records, 1867-1952
1870 Census
1871 Ohio, U.S., County Marriage Records, 1774-1993
1880 Census
1900 Census
1910 Census
1914 U.S., City Directories, 1822-1995
1915 Find A Grave

Jeremiah Soper (1837-)

Jeremiah Soper is listed in the 1850 census as 13 years old and living with William and Percy Soper. There are no further confirmed records for him.

Migration:
1850 Louisville, New York

Sources:
1850 Census

Electa Lake Soper (1838-)

Electa Soper is listed in the 1850 census as 12 years old and living with William and Percy Soper. There are no further confirmed records for her.

Migration:
1850 Louisville, New York

Sources:
1850 Census

Naomi Lavina Soper (1840-1914)

Naomi Lavina Soper (1840–1914) was born on March 10, 1840 in New York. She married Dewitt Clinton Palmer on October 10, 1858 in New York. They had 3 children. She spent most of her life in Michigan. Except for the 1900 census when she was living in South Dakota. In 1910 she returned to Michigan and is living with her younger brother William. She died in Quincy, Michigan on June 4, 1914 and is buried in Coldwater, Michigan.

There is a possible fourth child in Eva Palmer who is listed as a daughter along with her children being listed as grandchildren in the 1900 census, but Eva is not listed in the 1860 or 1870 census with the family. An Eva Palmer is listed in the 1860 census to Warren and Jane Palmer. She is most likely a niece to Naomi.

Migration:
1840 Brasher Falls, New York
1850 Louisville, New York
1860 Reading, MI
1900 Day, South Dakota
1910 Quincy, Michigan
1914 Quincy, Michigan

Children:
Carlton Palmer (1859–)
Franklin B Palmer (1862–1892)
Jefferson S. Palmer (1864–)

Sources:
1850 Census
1855 NY State Census
1860 Census
1870 Census
1880 Census
1900 Census
1910 Census
1914, Michigan, U.S., Death Records, 1897-1929 (Index)
1914, Michigan, Death Records, 1867-1950
1914 Find A Grave

Mary Melissa Soper (1841–1912)

Mary Melissa Soper (1841–1912) was born on June 14, 1841 in New York. She married Thomas Faulkner. They had 2 children, Martha (1860-?) and Emma (1867-1914). In the 1910 census she was listed as a widower. Her death record indicates she died on January 21, 1912 in Reading, Michigan.

According to Mary's daughter Emma's death record, Emma died by suicide with a gunshot to her right temple in 1914.

Migration:
1840 Brasher Falls, New York
1850 Louisville, New York
1860 Reading, MI
1900 Day, South Dakota
1910 Reading, Michigan
1912 Reading, Michigan

Children:
Martha Faulkner (1860-?)
Emma Faulkner (1867-1914)

Sources:
1850 Census
1855 NY State Census
1860 Census
1910 Census
1912, Michigan, U.S., Death Records, 1897-1929 (Index)
1912, Michigan, Death Records, 1867-1950
1912 Find A Grave
1914 Michigan, Death Records, 1867-1950 (Emma Faulkner)

William Henry Soper (1843–1923)

William Henry Soper (1843–1923) was born 1843 in New York. He married Rhoda Cornelia Kellogg (1839–1906). There are no records of any children. The 1900 census indicated they had been married for 24 years, however, Michigan marriage records indicate they were married May 29, 1871. In the 1910 census he was listed as a widower and living with his older sister Naomi in Quincy, Michigan. The 1920 census shows him living in Quincy, Michigan living by himself. He passed away on May 29, 1923 in Coldwater, Michigan and is buried there in Oak Grove Cemetery.

Migration:
1830 Fort Covington, New York
1840 Brasher Falls, New York
1850 Louisville, New York
1860 Reading, MI
1870 Quincy, Michigan
1923 Coldwater, Michigan

Sources:
1850 Census
1860 Census
1870 Census
Michigan, U.S., Marriage Records, 1867-1952
1880 Census
1900 Census
1910 Census
1920 Census
1923, Michigan, U.S., Death Records, 1897-1929 (Index)
1923, Michigan, Death Records, 1867-1950
1923 Find A Grave

Oliver C Soper (1845–)

Oliver C Soper (1845–) was born 1845 in New York. He married Mary A. Lammon (1853–) on August 15, 1875. They had 2 children. Oliver is listed as attending Jennings Seminary in Aurora, Illinois in 1872. Also listed on the same page is Joseph Soper of Quincy, Michigan. The date of his death and Mary's is unknown.

Migration:
1850 Louisville, New York
1860 Reading, Michigan
1872 Aurora, Illinois
1880 Jonesville, Michigan

Children:
Lettie Soper (1871–)
Gertie Soper (1877–)

Sources:
1850 Census
1855 NY State Census
1860 Census
1870 Census
1872 U.S., School Catalogs, 1765-1935
1875 Michigan, U.S., Marriage Records, 1867-1952
1880 Census

Rosette Chloe Soper (1847–1924)

Rosette Chloe Soper (1847–1924) was born on November 23, 1847 in New York. She married Asa Lindsley (1835-1917) on August 16, 1868. They had 5 children together and lived in Reading, Michigan until their deaths. Rosette died on May 8, 1824, and Asa Lindsley died in 1917.

Migration:
1850 Louisville, New York
1860 Reading, MI
1924 Reading, MI

Children:
Cora Alice Lindsley (1869– after 1950)
Edna Lindsley (1873–1925)
Myrtle Lindsley (1878–1906)
Arthur Lindsley (1880–1942)
Roy Lindsley (1883–1902)

Sources:
1850 Census
1855 New York Census
1860 Census
1870 Census
1880 Census
1900 Census
1910 Census
1920 Census
1924 Michigan, Death Records, 1867-1950

Joseph James Soper (1850–Aft. 1913)

Joseph James Soper (1850–Aft. 1913) was born in June 1850 in Louisville, New York. He can be seen in the 1855 NY census with his family. The 1860 census shows him in Reading, Michigan. There is an 1872 record of Joseph Soper at the Jennings Seminary in Aurora, Illinois at the same time his brother Oliver is there. He married Mary

Elizabeth Wingo on March 18, 1879 in Missouri. On the marriage record he is listed as Doct. Joseph J Soper of Chicago, Illinois. They had 5 children together. Two sons served in WWI, with Claude Clay Soper (1890-1918) dying in France of meningitis a month after the armistice. The 1880 Census shows them in Carroll, Missouri. Their son, Claude Clay Soper, was born in Montana in 1890. By 1900 they were in Seattle, Washington and in 1910 Bidwell, California. Mary died in California in 1913 and the date for Joseph's passing is currently unknown.

Migration:
1850 Louisville, New York
1860 Reading, Michigan
1880 Carroll, Missouri
1890 Montana
1900 Seattle, Washington
1910 Bidwell, California

Children:
Martha Melissa Soper (1879–1959)
James Henry Soper (1882–1952)
Claude Clay Soper (1890–1918)
Lola Carol Soper (1894–1973)
Lelia Soper (1897–1908)

Sources:
1850 Census
1855 New York Census
1860 Census
1879 Missouri, U.S., Compiled Marriages, 1851-1900 (Index)
1879 Missouri, U.S., Marriage Records, 1805-2002
1880 Census
1900 Census
1910 Census

Obituary Oroville Daily Register Oroville, California, July 3, 1913

Phoebe Elizabeth Soper (1853-1932)

Phoebe Elizabeth Soper (1853–1932) was born on November 21, 1853 in New York. She married Sylvester S. Bailey (1856-1935) on December 22, 1874 in Reading, Michigan. They had 2 children together. Mrtya/Myrtle Maude was born in 1876 but is only listed on the 1880 census. No further records were available. Phoebe passed away in Star, Michigan on February 18, 1932, and Sylvester passed away in 1935.

Migration:
1855 New York Census
1860 Reading, Michigan
1880 Adams, Michigan
1900 Star, Michigan
1932 Star, Michigan

Children:
Myrta Maude (1876-?)
Irma Bailey (1895-1930)

Sources:
1855 New York Census
1860 Census
1870 Census
1880 Census
1900 Census
1910 Census
1930 Census
1932 Michigan, Death Records, 1867-1950
1932 U.S., Find a Grave

Phoebe Soper (1810-?)

Phoebe Soper (1810-?) no further records have been identified.

Clarissa Soper (1811-1882)

Clarissa Soper (1811-1882) was born in Milton, Vermont on February 6, 1811. She was married twice, first to Jeremiah Conklin on April 6, 1831 in Bombay, New York. Jeremiah and Clarissa had 7 children together. Jeremiah passed away sometime before 1850 and Clarissa moved to Lake County with her children, though she is listed twice in the 1850 census. The NY census (8 Sep 1850) shows her living with her parents in the 1850 census in Lawrence, New York. She is also listed as residing with the Davidson family (23rd Sept 1850) in Libertyville, with her daughter Martha Conklin. Her 5 yr old daughter, Angeline, was listed as living with Clarissa's sister, Elizabeth Charity Pelton, in the 1850 census. Daughter Ann Marie was born in New York and in the 1850 census she is listed as 17 years old and living in Lake County with Edward and Julia Jones, Julia being Clarissa's younger sister.

Moses Johnson is listed in the 1850 census with his first wife, Harriet Johnson (age 30) and two children, Elijah Johnson (age 10) and Harriet Johnson (age 4) where they are living with Obadiah and Lucinda Crawford in Fremont. Moses and his family all hailed from New York. At some point his wife Harriet died leaving Moses with his two children. This would eventually lead to Clarissa marrying Moses Johnson in Lake County on June 12, 1854.

The 1860 census shows M. Conklin (age 23) as the head of the household and his occupation is listed as a farmer. This is likely Isaiah Martin Conklin, who often went by Martin and was born in 1837. We also can see Moses, Clarissa and Joseph Conklin, Martha Johnson (age 21) and Angeline Johnson (age 15). It is possible that Martha Johnson is actually Clarissa's daughter Martha Conklin as Moses is not listed as having a daughter named Martha or Angeline in the 1850 census and Clarissa has a Martha that was born in 1839 in New York. Further,

Angeline Johnson may actually be her youngest daughter, Angeline M Conklin, who was born in New York in 1845.

During the Civil War, Clarissa and her family would heed the call to serve against the rebellion. Clarissa's son, Joseph Conklin is the first family member to enlist in May 1861 serving for three years in the 15th Illinois Infantry Company I as a private before mustering out in May 1864. He would participate in the Battle of Shiloh, the Siege of Corinth, and the Siege of Vicksburg.

Soon after, her husband, Moses Johnson, step-son, Elijah Johnson, and son Isaiah Martin Conklin enlisted on the same date, April 26, 1862 serving in the 65th Illinois Infantry Company F, also known as the "Scotch Regiment". Elijah Johnson and Isaiah Martin Conklin would later re-enlist and be transferred to Company K, serving out the remainder of the war. Moses would be discharged for an unknown disability in September 1862. Elijah and Martin participated in the Atlanta Campaign, the March to the Sea, Kenesaw Mountain, Battle of Franklin and the Battle of Nashville.

Her oldest son, Jeremiah Conklin, enlisted in August 1862 into the 96th Illinois Infantry Company G but was discharged for disability in April 1863 in Brentwood, Teneesee. Clarissa's daughter, Ann Marie, would also know the worry of a husband serving in the war, as her husband Samuel Moore joined the 144th Illinois Infantry Company H in October 1864 serving out the remainder of the war. Samuel was assigned to guard duty on the Alton and St Louis Railroad in St Louis. While there he reputedly contracted typhoid fever which would affect him the rest of his life.

Joseph Conklin	15th Illinois Infantry Company I	May 24, 1861/ May 24, 1864	Battle of Shiloh, Siege of Corinth, Battle of Ft Donelson, and Siege of Vicksburg
Moses Johnson	65th Illinois Infantry Company F	April 26, 1862/ September 1, 1862	
Elijah Johnson	65th Illinois Infantry Company F/ Company K	April 26, 1862/ Re-enlist Apr 7, 1864/July 13, 1865	Atlanta Campaign, March to the Sea, Kenesaw Mountain, Battle of Franklin and the Battle of Nashville
Isaiah Martin Conklin	65th Illinois Infantry Company F/ Company K	April 26, 1862/ Re-enlist Apr 7, 1864/July 13, 1865	Atlanta Campaign, March to the Sea, Kenesaw Mountain, Battle of Franklin and the Battle of Nashville

| Jeremiah Conklin | 96th Illinois Infantry Company G | September 6, 1862/ Discharged April 1863 | |
| Samuel Moore | 144th Illinois Infantry Company H | October 18, 1864/July 14, 1865 | Ordered to St. Louis, Mo., and duty in that District till July, 1865. Regiment lost 69 to disease during service. |

When all was said and done, Clarissa would have a husband, all three of her sons, a step-son and a son-in-law serve the nation in the bloody conflict. Miraculously, all would survive the war, with Moses Johnson and Jeremiah Conklin receiving discharges for unspecified injuries.

After the war, brothers Jeremiah, Joseph, and Isaiah moved to Michigan where they married, and raised their families and eventually passed away. Martha Amanda Conklin (1839-1915) married her step-brother, Elijah Johnson in 1865 in Michigan, they would move back and forth between Michigan and Illinois over the ensuing years.

The 1880 census shows Clara Johnson living in Kansas City, Missouri with her grandchildren, Wilmont and Clara Pratt. Clarissa died on March 3, 1882 in Lake Forest, Illinois. Clarissa's 1882 obituary has a typo, omitting the last name of Soper and simply listing her parents as, Joseph and Electa Lake.

Migration:
1809 Milton, Vermont
1823 Bombay, New York
1830 Fort Covington, New York

1840 Brasher Falls, New York
1850 Lawrence, New York
1851 Lake County, Illinois
1880 Kansas City, MO
1882 Lake County, Illinois

Children:
Lovina Mary Conklin (1832-1884)
Ann Marie Conklin (1833-1908)
Jeremiah Conklin (1835-1905)
Isaiah Martin Conklin (1837-1902)
Martha Amanda Conklin (1839-1915)
Joseph Auburn Conklin (1842-1924)
Angeline M. Conklin (1845-1880)

Sources:
1850 Census, New York and IL
1850 Marriage Record
1860 Census
1870 Census
1880 Census
Portrait and Biographical Album of Lake County, Illinois 1891.
Page 486-487
"Clarissa Johnson Obituary" - The Waukegan Weekly Gazette - 18
Mar 1882
- Page 3
15th Illinois Infantry Regiment
https://civilwar.illinoisgenweb.org/history/015.html
https://en.wikipedia.org/wiki/15th_Illinois_Infantry_Regiment
http://www.civilwararchive.com/Unreghst/unilinf1.htm#15th
Joseph Conklin
https://apps.ilsos.gov/isaveterans/civilMusterSearch.do?key=50893
Elijah Johnson

https://apps.ilsos.gov/isaveterans/civilMuster-
Search.do?key=131144

https://apps.ilsos.gov/isaveterans/civilMuster-
Search.do?key=131145

Moses Johnson

https://apps.ilsos.gov/isaveterans/civilMuster-
Search.do?key=132050

65th Illinois Infantry Regiment

https://civilwar.illinoisgenweb.org/reg_html/065_reg.html

https://en.wikipedia.org/wiki/65th_Illinois_Infantry_Regiment

http://www.civilwararchive.com/Unreghst/unilinf6.htm#65th

Isaiah Conklin

https://apps.ilsos.gov/isaveterans/civilMusterSearch.do?key=50901

https://apps.ilsos.gov/isaveterans/civilMusterSearch.do?key=50902

https://apps.ilsos.gov/isaveterans/civilMusterSearch.do?key=50903

96th Illinois Infantry Regiment

https://civilwar.illinoisgenweb.org/r100/096-g-in.html

https://en.wikipedia.org/wiki/96th_Illinois_Volunteer_Infan-
try_Regiment

http://www.civilwararchive.com/Unreghst/unilinf8.htm#96th

Jeremiah Conklin

https://apps.ilsos.gov/isaveterans/civilMusterSearch.do?key=50883

144th Illinois Infantry Regiment

https://civilwar.illinoisgenweb.org/r155/144-h-in.html

https://en.wikipedia.org/wiki/144th_Illinois_Volunteer_Infan-
try_Regiment

http://www.civilwararchive.com/Unreghst/unilif11.htm#144th

Samuel Moore

https://apps.ilsos.gov/isaveterans/civilMuster-
Search.do?key=179020

Lovina Mary Conklin (1832-1884)

Lovina was born in New York on January 18, 1832. After traveling to Illinois from New York with her mother, Lovina was working for the Moody family and met Samuel Burris (1825-1911). They married on October 16, 1853 in Lake County, Illinois. Lovina would have 10 children with Samuel. Lovina passed away on May 13, 1884 in Waukegan, Illinois.

Migration:
1832 Fort Covington, New York
1840 Brasher Falls, New York
1850 Lawrence, New York
1851 Lake County, Illinois
1884 Lake County, Illinois

Children:
Orlando William Burris (1854–1927)
William Freemont Burris (1855–1908)
Harriett "Hattie" Lovina Burris (1859–1951)
Emma Marie Burris (1861–1930)
Caroline "Calla" May Burris (1863–1936)
Frank Delbert Burris (1865–1941)
Lindon Samuel Burris (1867–1885)
Jeremiah Lebeus Burris (1872–1929)
Estella Evelina Burris (1875–1876)

Sources:
1853 Marriage Record
1860 Census
1870 Census
1880 Census
1884 Find A Grave

Portrait and Biographical Album of Lake County, Illinois 1891. Page 710-711

Ann Marie Conklin (1833-1908)

Ann Marie was born in New York on April 24, 1832, and in the 1850 census she is listed as 17 years old and living in Lake County with Edward and Julia Jones. Julia is her mother's younger sister. Anne Marie married Samuel Moore (1829-1906) on October 25, 1851 in Lake County and had four children, one is believed to have died in infancy. Samuel served in the Civil War in the 144th Illinois Infantry, Company H where he did guard duty on the Alton and St Louis Railroad. He contracted typhoid fever which affected him the rest of his life and was discharged on July 20, 1865. Anne Marie died in Libertyville on December 31, 1908.

Migration:
1833 Fort Covington, New York
1840 Brasher Falls, New York
1850 Lawrence, New York
1850 Lake County, Illinois
1908 Lake County, Illinois

Children:
Judson Moore (1853-1930)
Willie A Moore (1855-1876)
Amanda Moore (1857-1880)

Sources:
1850 Census
1851 Marriage Record
1860 Census
1870 Census

1880 Census

Portrait and Biographical Album of Lake County, Illinois 1891. Page 488-489

1900 Census

"Obituary Ann M. Moore" Lake County Independent and Waukegan Weekly Sun - 8 Jan 1909 - Page 7

1908 Find A Grave

144th Illinois Infantry Regiment

https://civilwar.illinoisgenweb.org/r155/144-h-in.html

https://en.wikipedia.org/wiki/144th_Illinois_Volunteer_Infantry_Regiment

http://www.civilwararchive.com/Unreghst/unilif11.htm#144th

https://apps.ilsos.gov/isaveterans/civilMuster-Search.do?key=179020

Jeremiah Conklin (1835-1905)

Jeremiah was born in New York on March 3, 1835, and while living in Lake County as a farmer served in the Civil War as a private in the Illinois 96th Infantry. Records show he joined on August 9th, 1862 in Waukegan, Illinois and was mustered in Rockford, Illinois on September 6th, 1862. He was discharged for a disability on April 2, 1863 in Brentwood, Tennessee. He returned home after the war, moved to Michigan and in 1866 married Melissa Fuller in Grand Traverse County Michigan. They would have one child, Alice, live into adulthood. Jeremiah died in Arcadia Township, Michigan on January 23rd, 1905.

His brother, Isaiah, married Mellissa's sister, Mary Jane Fuller. Melissa and Mary Jane's mother was Sarah "Sally" Mansfield (1819-1874), the daughter of Amasa Mansfield (1792-1875) and Electa Soper (1792-1869) making them second cousins.

Migration:
1835 Fort Covington, New York

1840 Brasher Falls, New York
1850 Lawrence, New York
1850 Lake County, Illinois
1866 Grand Traverse County, MI
1905 Arcadia Township, MI

Children:
Clarrisa Conklin (1866-1866)
James M. Conklin (1866-1866)
Alice M. Conklin (1870-1906)

Sources:
1860 Census
1866 Marriage Record
1870 Census
1880 Census
1900 Census
1905 Death Record
1905 Find A Grave
96th Illinois Infantry Regiment
https://civilwar.illinoisgenweb.org/r100/096-g-in.html
https://en.wikipedia.org/wiki/96th_Illinois_Volunteer_Infan-
try_Regiment
http://www.civilwararchive.com/Unreghst/unilinf8.htm#96th
https://apps.ilsos.gov/isaveterans/civilMusterSearch.do?key=50883

Isaiah Martin Conklin (1837-1902)

Isaiah, who often went by Martin, was born in New York on May
21, 1837. Records show he served in the Civil War in the 65th Illinois
Infantry, Company K. He served nearly 4 years attaining the rank of
orderly sergeant. After the war he moved to Michigan and married Mary
Jane Fuller on Christmas Eve 1865 in the home of Moses Johnson in

Grand Traverse County Michigan. His brother, Jeremiah married Mary Jane's sister, Melissa Fuller. Isaiah and Mary Jane would have one child, Martin Roscoe Conklin. Isaiah died in Bear Lake, Michigan on April 26, 1902. Mary Jane died in Frankfort, Michigan in 1917.

His brother married Mary Jane's sister, Mellissa Fuller. Melissa and Mary Jane's mother was Sarah "Sally" Mansfield (1819-1874), the daughter of Amasa Mansfield (1792-1875) and Electa Soper (1792-1869) making them second cousins.

Migration:
1835 Fort Covington, New York
1840 Brasher Falls, New York
1850 Lawrence, New York
1850 Lake County, Illinois
1865 Grand Traverse County, MI
1902 Bear Lake, MI

Children:
Martin Roscoe Conklin (1877-?)

Sources:
1870 Census
1880 Census
1890 Veterans Schedules of the US Census
1900 Census
Civil War Pension Index: General Index to Pension Files, 1861-1934
Headstones Provided for Deceased Union Civil War Veterans, 1861-1904
1902 Death Record
1865 Marriage Record
"Another Veteran Passes Away" - Lake County Independent, Libertyville, Illinois, Friday, May 16, 1902. Page 5.
1902 Find A Grave

U.S., Selected Federal Census Non-Population Schedules, 1850-1880, 1870 enumeration date.

65th Illinois Infantry Regiment

https://civilwar.illinoisgenweb.org/reg_html/065_reg.html

https://en.wikipedia.org/wiki/65th_Illinois_Infantry_Regiment

http://www.civilwararchive.com/Unreghst/unilinf6.htm#65th

https://apps.ilsos.gov/isaveterans/civilMusterSearch.do?key=50901

https://apps.ilsos.gov/isaveterans/civilMusterSearch.do?key=50902

https://apps.ilsos.gov/isaveterans/civilMusterSearch.do?key=50903

Martha Amanda Conklin (1839-1915)

Martha was born in New York on March 12, 1839. In 1850 after her father Jeremiah died, Martha is listed in the 1850 census with her mother, Clarissa and living with the Davidson family in Libertyville, Illinois. Her mother remarried, to Moses Johnson in 1854. Martha married Civil War veteran and step brother, Elijah A. Johnson (1837-1909) on Christmas Eve 1865 in Grand Traverse County, Michigan, likely the same time as her brother Isaiah Martin Conklin married Mary Jane Fuller. During the war Elijah served in the 65th Illinois Volunteer Infantry.

She and Elijah later took up residence in Almira, Michigan. They would have five children together. By 1880, the family had moved back to Shields Township (Libertyville) Lake County, Illinois. In June 1900, however, they were back in Michigan living in Arcadia Township. They returned again to Lake County, Illinois and Elijah died in 1909 in Libertyville. In 1910 Martha is shown in the census living in Shields Township, Lake County, Illinois with her son Herman's family and she died in Libertyville on September 27, 1915.

Migration:
1835 Fort Covington, New York
1840 Brasher Falls, New York

1850 Lawrence, New York
1850 Lake County, Illinois
1865 Grand Traverse County, MI
1880 Lake County, Illinois
1900 Arcadia Township, MI
1909 Libertyville, Illinois
1915 Libertyville, Illinois

Children:
Herman Ulysses Grant Johnson (1867-1926)
Albert Johnson (1869-1880)
Rosteen W. Johnson (1870-1926)
Arthur Henry Johnson (1875-1976)
William Adelbert Johnson (1881-1933)

Sources:
1850 Census
1860 Census
1870 Census
1880 Census
1900 Census
Civil War Pension Index: General Index to Pension Files, 1861-1934
1910 Census
1915 Find A Grave
"Elijah Johnson obituary" Lake County Independent and Waukegan Weekly Sun Libertyville, Illinois, Friday, May 21, 1909. Page 4
"Smashes in Door; Finds His Mother Dead In Her Bed" - Lake County Independent and Waukegan Weekly Sun Libertyville, Illinois, Friday, October 1, 1915. Page 7.
65th Illinois Infantry Regiment
https://civilwar.illinoisgenweb.org/reg_html/065_reg.html
https://en.wikipedia.org/wiki/65th_Illinois_Infantry_Regiment
http://www.civilwararchive.com/Unreghst/unilinf6.htm#65th

https://apps.ilsos.gov/isaveterans/civilMuster-
Search.do?key=131144

https://apps.ilsos.gov/isaveterans/civilMuster-
Search.do?key=131145

Joseph Auburn Conklin (1842-1924)

Joseph was born in New York on April 14, 1842. As with his brothers, he served in the Civil War in the 15th Illinois Infantry Company I. After the war, he would marry Orpha Alvira Pratt on June 11, 1865 in Grand Traverse County, Michigan. Orpha was from St Lawrence County, New York. They lived in Michigan and had nine children together. Joseph died on December 3, 1924 in Frankfort, MI. Orpha passed away in Frankfort in 1934.

Migration:
1842 Brasher Falls, New York
1850 Lawrence, New York
1850 Lake County, Illinois
1865 Grand Traverse County, MI
1924 Frankfort, MI

Children:
Emma W. Conklin (1866–1935)
Algernon "Algie" Conklin (1869–1870)
Lillian "Lilly" M. Conklin (1871–1909)
Edith Jocellyn "Josie" Conklin (1873–1965)
Jolina Conklin (1873–)
Jeremiah "Jeb" Orpheus Conklin (1875–1936)
Clifford Algernon Conklin (1877–1951)
Howard Conklin (1881–1881)
Hazel Conklin (1886–1887)

Sources:

1860 Census

"Lake County Union Rifle Guards" The Waukegan Weekly Gazette, Waukegan, Illinois, 04 May 1861. Page 3

1865 Marriage Record

1870 Census

1880 Census

1900 Census

1910 Census

1920 Census

1924 Death Record

1924 Find A Grave

1924 U.S., Headstone Applications for Military Veterans, 1925-1963

1924 Civil War Pension Index: General Index to Pension Files, 1861-1934

15th Illinois Infantry Regiment

https://civilwar.illinoisgenweb.org/history/015.html

https://en.wikipedia.org/wiki/15th_Illinois_Infantry_Regiment

http://www.civilwararchive.com/Unreghst/unilinf1.htm#15th

https://apps.ilsos.gov/isaveterans/civilMusterSearch.do?key=50893

Angeline M. Conklin (1845-1873)

Angeline was born in 1845 in Brashar, New York. In 1850 after the death of her father a five year old Angeline Conklin was living with her aunt and uncle, Elizabeth Charity (Soper) Pelton and Steven Pelton. In 1865 she married Stephen Pratt (1833-1915) in Traverse City, Michigan. They had two children together, Wilmont Adelbert "Del" Pratt (1866–1936) and Clara A Pratt (1869–1901). Efforts to find Angeline in the 1870 census have not been successful. It is believed Angeline passed away in Michigan prior to 1873, when Stephen remarried to Mary St John in December of 1873 but it is possible she may have divorced and lived until 1879-1880 before the 1880 census.

Stephen and Mary had two children live into adulthood, Caroline Pratt (1874-1917) and Emma Pratt (1874-1918). On January 7, 1880 Mary had a stillborn son and two weeks later she died on January 21, 1880. The 1880 census shows Stephen and his daughter Caroline living as boarders with the Vaughan family in Inland, Michigan. Stephen's mother is also listed as a boarder. The 1880 census appears to show that Josiah and Rachel Gray adopted Emma after the death of her mother in early 1880.

Stephen's oldest two children, Wilmont Pratt and Clara Pratt are listed in the 1880 census as living in Kansas with their maternal grandmother, Clarissa (Soper) Johnson.

Stephen married a third time to Emma Smith (1842-1917) possibly in 1888. The 1900 census listed Stephen, Mary and their daughter, Edith (1890-1975) living in Little Falls, Wisconsin. Note, there is an error in the census form for how many years they are married. Stephen passed away in 1915 and his third wife, Emma passed in 1917.

Migration:
1845 Brasher Falls, New York
1850 Lawrence, New York
1850 Lake County, Illinois
1865 Grand Traverse County, MI
1879 Almira, MI

Children:
Wilmont Adelbert "Del" Pratt (1866–1936)
Clara A Pratt (1869–1901)

Sources:
1850 Census
1860 Census
1865 Marriage Record

Pratt-St John Wedding Announcement - Grand Traverse Herald December 11, 1873
Michigan, U.S., Wills and Probate Records, 1784-1980
Grand Traverse County, Michigan, U.S., Marriage Index, 1853-2012
1880 Census

Naomi Lovina Soper (1813-1884)

Naomi Lovina Soper (1813-1884) was born in Milton, Vermont on July 15, 1813. She married Abram Kasler (1806-1891) and settled in Ohio where they had 11 children. The 1850 and 1860 census shows them living in Homer, Ohio. The 1870 census lists them in Ames, Ohio and In 1880 they are back in Homer, Ohio. Naomi died on October 29, 1884 and is buried in Athens, Ohio. Abram died in 1891.

There is an 1850 census listing in St Lawrence County, New York that shows a 36 year old Noama Soper living with Joseph Soper and family. There is also an Ohio census listing Abram Kasler and Lavina Kasler with their family in Homer, Ohio.

Migration:
1809 Milton, Vermont
1823 Bombay, New York
1830 Fort Covington, New York
1840 Brasher Falls, New York
1850 Homer, Ohio

Children:
John M Kasler (1835–1887)
Miranda Kasler (1836–1910)
Joseph S. Kasler (1837–1904)
James William Kasler (1840–1890)
George M. Kasler (1841–1910)
Clarissa Electa Kasler (1845–)
Washington Linsey Kasler (1847–1932)

Perley Nelson Kasler (1849–1927)
Mary Angeline Kasler (1851–1888)
Elizabeth Kasler (1854–1893)
David Eli Kasler (1856–1882)

Sources:
1850 Census
1860 Census
1870 Census
1880 Census
1884 Find A Grave

John M Kasler (1835-1887)

John M Kasler (1835–1887) was born on December 10, 1835 in New York. He married Samantha Tryon on August 9, 1868 in Morgan County, Ohio. The 1870 census lists them living in Butler, Missouri and by 1880 they returned to Homer, Ohio. John died on April 7, 1887 and is buried in Bishopville Cemetery. Samantha remarried in 1893 to William Jackson "W.J." Chambers, and died on January 14, 1919.

Migration:
1835 Fort Covington, New York
1850 Homer, Ohio
1860 Homer, Ohio
1870 Butler, Missouri
1880 Homer, Ohio
1887 Ohio

Sources:
1850 Census
1860 Census
1868 Ohio, U.S., County Marriage Records, 1774-1993

1870 Census
1880 Census
1880 U.S., Selected Federal Census Non-Population Schedules, 1850-1880
1887 Find A Grave

Miranda Kasler (1836–1910)

Miranda Kasler (1836–1910) was born on January 22, 1836, in New York. By the 1850 Census she was living with her family in Homer, Ohio. She married John Morris Keirns (1836-1880) on September 6, 1858 in Athens County, Ohio. They had one son, John Acel Keirns (1860-1901). The 1870 census lists them living in Ames, Ohio. John Morris died on September 13, 1880. The 1900 census shows Miranda living with her son and daughter in-law, Margaret. In 1910 Miranda is listed as living with her daughter in-law, Margaret in Ames. She died on August 8, 1910, and is buried in Hooper Ridge Cemetery in Amesville, Ohio.

Migration:
1836 Fort Covington, New York
1850 Homer, Ohio
1860 Homer, Ohio
1870 Ames, Ohio
1910 Ames, Ohio

Children:
John Acel Keirns (1860-1901)

Sources:
1850 Census
1858 Ohio, U.S., County Marriage Records, 1774-1993
1860 Census

1870 Census
1880 Census
1900 Census
1910 Census
1910 Find A Grave

Joseph S. Kasler (1837–1904)

Joseph S. Kasler (1837–1904) was born on March 25, 1837, in New York. By the 1850 Census he was living with his family in Homer, Ohio. He married Elizabeth J. Standley (1840-1907) on November 8 1857 Morgan, Ohio.

According to the 1890 Veterans Schedules of the U.S. Federal Census Joseph served as a private in the 53rd Ohio Infantry, Company G. He enlisted on October 28 1861 and was discharged on August 11, 1865. He appears to have been enlisted for most of the war and his unit was in many notable engagements.

The 1860 census listed a young James Valentine living with them in Homer, Ohio. The 1870 census lists them living in Ward, Ohio and the 1880 Census lists them living in Trimble, Ohio. The 1900 census James and Elizabeth are living in Salt Lick, Ohio. He died on January 13, 1904 and is buried in Bishopville Cemetery. Elizabeth passed away on March 9, 1907 in Congo, Ohio and is also buried in Bishopville Cemetery.

Migration:
1837 Fort Covington, New York
1850 Homer, Ohio
1860 Homer, Ohio
1870 Ward, Ohio
1880 Trimble, Ohio
1890 Monroe and Corning, Ohio
1900 Salt Lick, Ohio
1904 Ohio

Children:

James Valentine Kasler (1859–1947)

Miranda Josephine Kasler (1861–1918)

Amy Lovina Kasler (1866–1947)

Sarah Alice Kasler (1868–1942)

Cora Dela Kasler (1871–1952)

Mary Electa Kasler (1874–1951)

Viola Blanche Kasler (1876–1957)

Sources:

1850 Census

1857 Ohio, U.S., County Marriage Records, 1774-1993

1870 Census

1880 Census

1890 Veterans Schedules of the U.S. Federal Census

1900 Census

1904 Find A Grave

U.S., Civil War Pension Index: General Index to Pension Files, 1861-1934

53rd Ohio Infantry, Co G

1887 John E. Stewart Civil War Veteran "In the Rifle Pits" Narrow Escape #11 Ironton Register 27 Jan. 1887 - https://lawrencecounty-ohio.com/military/john-e-stewart-civil-war-veteran/

1887 Peter Kingry Civil War Veteran "Who Killed General Johnson?" Narrow Escape #21

Ironton Register 7 April 1887 - https://lawrencecountyohio.com/military/peter-kingry-civil-war-veteran/

http://www.ohiocivilwar.com/cw53.html

See the wikipedia page for a list of their engagements: https://en.wikipedia.org/wiki/53rd_Ohio_Infantry_Regiment

James William Kasler (1840-1890)

Joseph S. Kasler (1837–1904) was born on October 5, 1841, in Morgan County, Ohio. By the 1850 Census he was living with his family in Homer, Ohio. He married Sarah Ellen Payne (1846-1901) on October 2, 1866 in Athens, Ohio.

The 1860 census he was still with his family in Homer, Ohio. The 1870 census lists them living in Dover, Ohio and the 1880 Census lists them living in Tucker, West Virginia. He died on July 26, 1890 and is buried in Bishopville Cemetery. Sarah passed away on December 7, 1901 and is also buried in Bishopville Cemetery.

Migration:
1841 Morgan County, Ohio
1850 Homer, Ohio
1860 Homer, Ohio
1870 Ward, Ohio
1880 Trimble, Ohio
1890 Monroe and Corning, Ohio
1900 Salt Lick, Ohio
1904 Ohio

Children:
Abram Kasler (1867–1936)
Mary E Kasler (1869–1888)
Emma Jane Kasler (1871–1947)
James Kasler (1874–1939)
Lydia S. "LoVanche" Kasler (1876–1927)
Charles Kasler (1879–1950)
Grace Lula Kasler (1882–1965)

Sources:
1850 Census

1860 Census
1866 Ohio, U.S., County Marriage Records, 1774-1993
1870 Census
1876 West Virginia, U.S., Births Index, 1804-1938 (Lydia Kasler)
1880 Census
1890 Find A Grave
1965 The Times Recorder, Zanesville, Ohio · Friday, January 08, 1965 Grace Kasler obituary)

George M. Kasler (1841–1910)

George M. Kasler (1841–1910) was born in 1843 in Ohio. In the 1850 Census he was living with his family in Homer, Ohio. The 1860 census shows him still with his family in Homer, Ohio. The 1870 census lists him in Ames, Ohio and the 1880 Census lists him living in Homer, Ohio again. In 1900 he was living with his brother Washington and his brother's family. He died on April 13, 1910 and is buried in Bishopville Cemetery. There are no records of George marrying or having children.

Migration:
1841 Morgan County, Ohio
1850 Homer, Ohio
1860 Homer, Ohio
1870 Ames, Ohio
1875 Homer, Ohio
1910 Homer Ohio

Sources:
1850 Census
1850 U.S., Selected Federal Census Non-Population Schedules, 1850-1880
1860 Census
1863 U.S., Civil War Draft Registrations Records, 1863-1865

1870 Census
1875 U.S., Indexed County Land Ownership Maps, 1860-1918
1880 Census
1900 Census
1910 Ohio, U.S., Death Records, 1908-1932, 1938-2018
1910 Find A Grave

Clarissa Electa Kasler (1845–?)

Clarissa Electa Kasler (1845–?) was born on November 11, 1845, in Ohio. She was married three times and there are no records of her having any children. Her first marriage was on January 15, 1864 to William Harkins (1843-1864). William served during the Civil War in the Ohio 9th Cavalry K Company where he is listed as dying of disease in December 1864.

Clarissa remarried on November 26, 1865 to Samuel Angel (1832-1884). Angel died in 1884 and is buried in Bishopville Cemetery. He was previously married to Elizabeth Ann Wogan (1831–1864) from 1850 until her death in 1864.

Clarissa married once more in 1885 to Jacob Jones (1836-?). There are no burial or death records of either Jacob Jones or Clarissa available at this time.

Migration:
1845 Ohio
1850 Homer, Ohio
1870 Ward, Ohio
1880 Ames, Ohio

Sources:
1850 Census
1860 Census

1864 Ohio, U.S., County Marriage Records, 1774-1993

1865 Civil War Pension Index: General Index to Pension Files, 1861-1934

1865 Ohio, U.S., County Marriage Records, 1774-1993

1870 Census

1880 Census

1885 Ohio, U.S., County Marriage Records, 1774-1993

Washington Linsey Kasler (1847–1932)

Washington Linsey Kasler (1847–1932) was born in 1847 in Ohio. He was married on February 11, 1875 to Susannah Burtnett. They had four children together. Washington would stay in and around Homer, Ohio for most of his life. His wife Susannah died in 1922 and is buried in Bishopville Cemetery. By the 1930 Census he was living with his daughter Muriel and her family in Murray City, Ohio. He died on January 31, 1932, and is buried in Bishopville Cemetery.

Migration:
1847 Ohio
1850 Homer, Ohio
1870 Ames, Ohio
1880 Homer, Ohio
1930 Murray City, Ohio

Children:
Wallace David Kasler (1879–1902)
Ethel Eva Kasler (1887–1990)
Mary Ida Kasler (1887–1893)
Muriel Gladys Kasler (1891–1985)

Sources:
1850 Census

1860 Census
1870 Census
1875 Ohio, U.S., County Marriage Records, 1774-1993
1880 Census
1900 Census
1910 Census
1920 Census
1930 Census
1932 Ohio Deaths, 1908-1932, 1938-1944, and 1958-2007
1932 U.S., Find A Grave Index, 1600s-Current

Mary Angeline Kasler (1848–1888)

Mary Angeline Kasler (1848–1888) was born in 1851 in Ohio. She was married on January 1, 1870 to Henry Clay Angle (1851-1945). They had eight children together. Mary would stay in Ohio for her entire life. She passed away in 1888 and her husband, Henry died in 1945. She is buried in Murray City Cemetery.

Migration:
1851 Homer, Ohio
1870 Hocking, Ohio
1880 Ames, Ohio
1888 Murray City, Ohio

Children:
Ida D Angle (1872–1930)
Dora A Angle (1873–1887)
Clarissa Electa Angle (1876–1950)
John R Angle (1879–1946)
Joseph Elbert Angle (1881–1953)
Bertus Raymond Angle (1884–1966)
Maude May Angle (1886–1942)

Frank Angle (1888–1952)

Sources:
1860 Census
1870 Census
1870 Ohio, U.S., County Marriage Records, 1774-1993
1880 Census
1888 Find A Grave

Purley Nelson Kasler (1849-1927)

Purley Nelson Kasler (1849–1927) was born on March 12, 1849, in Ohio. He was married on November 10, 1870, to Sarah Katherine Swett (1849-1922). They had eight children together. Purley would stay in Ohio for his entire life. His wife Sarah died in 1922 and Purley passed away on July 11, 1927. He is buried in Glouster Cemetery.

Migration:
1849 Ohio
1850 Homer, Ohio
1870 Ames, Ohio
1880 Ward, Ohio
1910 Trimble, Ohio
1927 Trimble, Ohio

Children:
Arza James Kasler (1871–1960)
Sarah Lavina Kasler (1873–1943)
Luetta Kasler (1876–1943)
William Kasler (1878–1965)
Addie Belle Kasler (1881–1948)
Arthur Clarence Kasler (1884–1956)
Harley Kasler (1886–1886)

Elizabeth Ann Kasler (1890–1890)

Sources:
1850 Census
1860 Census
1870 Census
1870 Ohio, U.S., County Marriage Records, 1774-1993
1880 Census
1910 Census
1920 Census
1927 Ohio, U.S., Death Records, 1908-1932, 1938-2018
1927 U.S., Find A Grave Index, 1600s-Current

Elizabeth Ann Kasler (1854–?)

Elizabeth Kasler (1854–?) was born in 1854 in Ohio. She was married to James Johnson (1851-?). They had four children together. It is currently unknown when she and her husband died and where they are buried.

Migration:
1854 Homer, Ohio
1870 Ames, Ohio
1880 Homer, Ohio

Children:
Mary Emily Johnson (1875–)
David E. Johnson (1879–)
Hettie G. Johnson (1879–1963)
Charles E Johnson (1885–1943)

Sources:
1860 Census

1870 Census
1870 Ohio, U.S., County Marriage Records, 1774-1993
1880 Census

David Eli Kasler (1856–1882)

David Eli Kasler (1856–1882) was born on March 9, 1856, in Ohio. He was married to Arrissa Lois Love (1857-1919) on February 8, 1877. They had two children together. David would stay in Ohio for his entire life and died at the young age of 26 on December 26, 1882. He is buried in Bishopville Cemetery.

Migration:
1856 Homer, Ohio
1870 Ames, Ohio
1877 Morgan, Ohio
1880 Homer, Ohio

Children:
Charles Harmon Kasler (1878–1961)
Eva Lena Kasler (1880–1904)

Sources:
1850 Census
1860 Census
1870 Census
1877 Ohio, U.S., County Marriage Records, 1774-1993
1880 Census
1882 Find A Grave

Joseph Miles Soper (1815-1891)

Joseph Miles Soper (1815-1891) was born in Milton, Vermont on July 17, 1815. In 1821 his family moved to Franklin County, New

York. Being heavily timbered, young Joseph worked hard clearing land and making potash and pearlash. In 1836 he married Angeline Gray (1820-1868). They had four children together. The 1840 and 1850 census shows Joseph living with his family in St Lawrence County, New York.

The "History of Franklin and Cerro Gordo counties, Iowa" states that he moved to Lake County, Illinois in 1851, staying there for two years. By 1851 Joseph had several siblings: Clarissa (Soper) Conklin, later Johnson (1811-1884), Mary Melissa (Soper) Gray (1820-1852), Elizabeth Charity (Soper) Pelton (1829-1904), Julia (Soper) Jones (1830-1884?), Sarah Louisa (Soper) Cramer (1832-1909) living in Lake County. He moved on to Buchanan County, Iowa after obtaining some land patents through the Bureau of Land Management. In 1853, two 40 acre parcels were obtained under the Scrip Warrant Act of 1850 and assigned to Joseph Miles on August 1, 1853. The first parcel (MW-0686-403) was obtained from Frederick Stahl for his service in Captain Stephensons Company Illinois Militia during the Black Hawk War. The second 40 acre parcel was obtained from his uncle, Remember Soper (1794-1872), for his service in Captain Mansfield's Company Vermont Militia during the War of 1812. Additionally there is a June 15, 1855 record of Miles Soper obtaining a land patent for 43 1/10 acres under the April, 1820 Land Act in Buchanan County.

The 1856 Iowa census and 1860 census shows Joseph living in Iowa with his family. He bought and moved onto a farm in Reeve Township where he became one of the pioneers of Franklin County. His first wife, Angeline, died at the age of 47 on September 30, 1868.

Angeline's sister, Abigail (Gray) Smith (1823-1880) had been widowed the year before when her husband Sanford Smith (1817-1867) died in Wisconsin. Joseph and Abigail were married three months after Angeline's death on December 23, 1868 in Franklin County, Iowa. It should be noted that Joseph's younger sister, Mary Melissa Soper (1820-1852) married Angeline and Abigail's older brother, Charles Gray.

Abigail passed away in 1880 and is buried in Franklin County, Iowa. Joseph would not wait long to marry again and married Rowenna Wood on January 24, 1881 in Franklin County, Iowa. Their marriage certificate lists Joseph and Electa as his parents. He lived for nearly 33 years on the Reeves Township farm. He later moved to Geneva where Joseph passed away on May 22, 1891. He is buried in the Maysville Cemetery.

Migration:
1809 Milton, Vermont
1823 Bombay, New York
1830 Fort Covington, New York
1840 Brasher Falls, New York
1850 Lawrence, New York
1851 Lake County, Illinois
1853 Buchanan County, Iowa
1856 Alton, Iowa
1860 Reeve, Iowa
1891 Geneva, Iowa

Children:
George Wesley Soper (1837–1925)
Hannah Lavina Soper (1840–1888)
William Wallace Soper (1842–1897)
Albert Miles Soper (1855–1925)

Sources:
1840 Census
1850 Census
1853 Scrip Warrant Act of 1850. MW-0686-404 and MW-0686-403. Retrieved from https://glorecords.blm.gov/search/
1855 - 1820 Land Act Wikipedia. https://en.wikipedia.org/wiki/Land_Act_of_1820

Land Patent Miles Soper 15 June 1855. Patent IA Vol 148 pg. 11. Retrieved from https://glorecords.blm.gov/search/

1856 Iowa Census

1860 Census

1868 Marriage Record

1870 Census

1880 Census

1881 Iowa, Marriage Records, 1880-1937, Iowa State Archives; Des Moines, Iowa; Volume: 302 (Dubuque - Henry)

1881 "History of Buchanan County, Iowa". Cleveland, Williams brothers. 1881 Retrived from https://archive.org/details/historyof-buchana00will/page/306/mode/2up - 15 Jan 2023

1883 "History of Franklin and Cerro Gordo counties, Iowa" Retrieved from https://archive.org/details/historyoffrankli01unio 5 March 2022

1891 Transcribed Obituary - Franklin Recorder - 5/27/1891 Retrieved from http://www.maysvilleiowa.com/whoswho/jmsoper.htm on 1 Jan 2022.

1891 Find A Grave

George Wesley Soper (1837–1925)

George was born in Brasher Falls, New York, on January 23, 1837. George married Constantinia M. Leggett in 1857, the ceremony was performed by Judge James B. Reeve. They had six children together and she died in 1871. On January 22, 1873 he married Ella M. Brown in Ohio and they had four children together.

By the 1860 Census, George was living with his family in Reeve, Iowa. During the Civil War, George served as a private for six months in 1861 in the Third Battery Iowa Light Artillery. After the war in the 1870 and 1880 census he was still in Reeve, Iowa. The 1900 census shows George living in Hampton, Iowa. The 1910 census he was living in Stanley, South Dakota with his wife, Ella. On March 4, 1925, George passed away in Dumont, Iowa and is buried in Hampton Cemetery.

Migration:
1840 Brasher Falls, New York
1850 Lawrence, New York
1851 Lake County, Illinois
1853 Buchanan County, Iowa
1856 Alton, Iowa
1860 Reeve, Iowa
1900 Hampton, Iowa

Children:
With Constantia
Florence A Soper (1858-1943)
Ella M Soper (1864-1949)
Charles M Soper (1866-1953)
Cora A Soper (1859-1902)
LuVerne W Soper (1872-1934)
Orville Soper (1870-1875)
With Ella
Constantia Emma Soper (1874-1951)
Jessie Mildred Soper (1876-1952)
Wallace Wilder Soper (1879-1952)
Leaverett Irving Soper (1880-1961)

Sources:
1850 Census
1856 Iowa Census
1870 Census
1883 "History of Franklin and Cerro Gordo counties, Iowa" Retrieved from https://archive.org/details/historyoffrankli01unio 5 March 2022

1900 Census
1910 Census
1918 U.S., Army Transport Service Arriving and Departing Passenger Lists, 1910-1939 (Wallace Soper, WWI record)
Iowa, U.S., Death Records, 1880-1904, 1921-1951
1925 Find A Grave

Hannah Lovina Soper (1840–1888)

Hannah was born in Brasher, New York on September 18, 1840. On April 2, 1858 Hannah married Colonel Arthur Tappan Reeve, brother of Franklin County's first judge James B. Reeve. Reeve was born in New Lyme, Ashtabula County in Ohio on Dec. 18, 1835. His grandfather and 3 brothers served in the Revolutionary War. He grew up on a farm and became a lawyer. He moved to Maysville, Iowa in 1854. In 1858, he attempted to make a claim in Buena Vista County but lost it and returned to Franklin County. He spent the summer of 1860 in the mines of Pike's Peak.

By 1861 Arthur met John Brown Jr. in Chicago and enlisted in the 7th regiment Kansas Cavalry (Jayhawkers). Arthur and Hannah would later name a son, John Brown Soper. Arthur served 18 months as a private then later as a non-commissioned officer. As African Americans entered service he was detailed to organize those troops. He had a company made ready in Corinth, Mississippi for the 55th Regiment Colored Infantry. Later he helped organize the 88th regiment Colored Infantry and was appointed major and subsequently Lieutenant Colonel. Later again, he helped organize another colored regiment and was made its colonel. He served as the first chief of the Freedmen's Bureau until January 1866, when he returned to Maysville and served as a member of the board of regents of the state university. He went to Washington DC as head of the seed division of the Department of Agriculture where he passed away on October 25, 1889. Hannah passed away earlier in the year on April 9, 1889, in Hampton, Iowa. They are both buried in Hampton Cemetery.

Twins Lula M. Reeve (1872-1928) and Lena A Reeve (1872-1910) moved to Washington DC. Lula married William Hoover, president of the National Trust and Savings Bank of Washington DC. She served as treasurer general of the Daughters of the American Revolution 1909-1913. Lena married A.W. Shunk who was the Chief of Division in the Adjutant General's office in Washington DC.

Migration:
1840 Brasher Falls, New York
1850 Lawrence, New York
1851 Lake County, Illinois
1853 Buchanan County, Iowa
1856 Alton, Iowa
1860 Reeve, Iowa
1870 Hampton, Iowa
1880 Hampton, Iowa

Children:
John Brown Reeve (1860-1923)
Ettie Geraldine Reeve (1863-1940)
Effie A Reeve (1868-1945)
Delos Norton Reeve (1869-1925)
Lula M. Reeve (1872-1928)
Lena A Reeve (1872-1910)

Sources:
1850 Census
1856 Iowa Census
1860 Census
U.S., Colored Troops Military Service Records, 1863-1865
1870 Census

1880 Census

1883 "History of Franklin and Cerro Gordo counties, Iowa" Retrieved from https://archive.org/details/historyoffrankli01unio 5 March 2022

1918 "Iowa : its history and its foremost citizens" Chicago : S. J. Clarke. Retrieved from

https://archive.org/details/iowaitshistoryit01brig

William Wallace Soper (1842–1897)

William was born February 18, 1842 in Brasher, New York. He moved west with his family eventually settling in Reeve, Iowa. William ran for coroner in 1860 but lost to L Shroyer. He helped organize the Alba Lodge No. 213 Odd Fellows lodge in Maysville on January 23, 1871. He eventually served as a Noble Grand for the lodge. He married Mary Elizabeth Newman on November 9, 1875. They had nine children together.

William moved with his wife and family to Los Angeles, California around 1882 and Pomona, California in 1883 according to Mary's obituary. He appeared in the Los Angeles County voter rolls in 1896. He passed away on 19 October 1897. His wife Mary passed away in 1902.

Migration:
1842 Brasher Falls, New York
1850 Lawrence, New York
1851 Lake County, Illinois
1853 Buchanan County, Iowa
1856 Alton, Iowa
1860 Reeve, Iowa
1880 Portlandville, Iowa
1882 Los Angeles, California
1883 Pomona, California

Children:
Ethel Ernestine Soper (1876–1959)
Edna May Soper (1879–1962)
Lorene Vivian Soper (1881–1909)
Arthur Orlando Soper (1883–1938)
Alice Lillian Soper (1885–1958)
Bernice Clair Soper (1887–1948)
Ernest Wallace Soper (1889–1961)
Helen Phoebe Dottie Soper (1892–1986)
Mary Evelyn Soper (1895–1953)

Sources:
1860 Census
1870 Census
1875 Marriage Record
1880 Census
1896 California, U.S., Voter Registers, 1866-1898
1897 Find A Grave
1902 The Pomona Progress, Pomona, California, 11 Jan 1902, Mary's obituary

Albert Miller Soper (1855-1925)

Albert was born in Alton, Iowa October 8, 1855. By the 1860 census he was in Reeve, Iowa and would stay in the area the remainder of his life. On April 8, 1876 he married Carrie Bangs (1855-1940) in Maysville. They had two children together. He died in 1925 and he is buried in Hampton Cemetery.

Migration:
1855 Alton, Iowa
1860 Reeve, Iowa
1925 Reeve, Iowa

Children:
Cecil Ione Soper (1882-1954)
Albert M Soper (1884-1938)

Sources:
1860 Census
1870 Census
1876 Iowa, Select Marriages Index, 1758-1996
1880 Census
1900 Census
1910 Census
1920 Census

Isaiah Martin Soper (1817-1861)

Not much is known about Isaiah Martin Soper (1817-1861) Some sources have Isaiah Martin Soper (1817-1861) serving in the Civil War and dying in the first Battle of Bull Run in Manassas, VA in 1861.

Mary Melissa Soper (1820-1852)

Mary Melissa Soper (1820-1852) was born in Brasher Falls, New York on November 2, 1820. She married Charles Gray (1817-1886) in New York likely sometime around 1842-1844 based on the birth of her oldest child Angeline. She appears only by her married name with Charles in the 1850 census. According to her oldest daughter, Angeline's 1925 obituary, her family moved to Lake County in 1848, when she was 4, which is likely incorrect since she was listed in Brasher Falls in the 1850 census. Angeline's death certificate lists her mothers name as Mary Soper, which is hard to read as the Soper was slightly overwritten.

Charles Gray and Mary Melissa Soper had five children. Only three daughters would live into adulthood. After the death of her mother the youngest child, Sarah Louisa Gray, would eventually be adopted by Stephen and Elizabeth Pelton. Elizabeth was her mother's younger sister.

Sarah Louisa Gray died in August 1860 and is listed as Sarah Louisa Pelton and buried in Diamond Lake Cemetery. Joseph Gray, age 4 is buried in Diamond Lake Cemetery with his mother. Mary's headstone was likely replaced or added at a later date. Compare the headstone for Sarah and Mary and you will see that they are not from the same era.

According to Diamond Lake Cemetery records, Charles Gray bought 4 grave plots in 1852 after the death of his wife. She is in one of the plots with Joseph, Sarah Louisa (Gray) Pelton is in another one. The last two plots would not be used until the death of Robert Dallas Laycock in 1942 and Marvin Laycock in 1979.

Charles Gray would remarry, Mary Gilder, on September 20, 1854 in Lake County, Illinois. By the 1856 Iowa census we find Charles' daughter, Angeline Gray, living in Alton, Iowa with Simon Cramer and Sarah Louisa (Soper) Cramer, her aunt and uncle. Also in 1856 we find 9 year old Harriet Gray living with Joseph Miles Soper and his family in Alton, Iowa.

In the 1857 Minnesota census we see Charles has brought his extended family together, if only for a short time. The 1857 Minnesota Census lists Angeline Gray, Mary Melissa Gray, Harriet Gray, and Sarah Gray with their half siblings, Jeanette and Theodore Gray. By the time of the 1860 census Charles' daughters with Mary Melissa (Soper) Gray were no longer living with him in Minnesota.

1860 Census data has not been found for Angeline Gray and Mary Melissa Gray. Given that Mary Melissa Gray married Eli Miller (1823-1874), on January 4, 1862 in Adel, Iowa, it is possible she was living somewhere in Iowa at the time of the 1860 census. A 12 year old Harriet Gray can be found on the 1860 census back in Iowa with her uncle, Joseph Miles Soper and his wife Angelina. Note Angelina is sister to Charles Gray, Harriet's father.

In 1860 Sarah Louisa was living with her adopted parents Stephen and Elizabeth (Soper) Pelton. It's believed she passed away some time after the July date of the 1860 census and before October 1860 when her adopted father Stephen wrote his will. The only child mentioned in the will is their other adopted child, George Pelton.

Charles served in the Minnesota Infantry during the Civil War and raised another family with Mary Gilder, mostly in Minnesota. He died in 1886 and is buried in Fairview Cemetery in Stillwater, Minnesota.

Migration:
1809 Milton, Vermont
1823 Bombay, New York
1830 Fort Covington, New York
1840 Brasher Falls, New York
1851 Lake County, Illinois

Children:
Angeline Charlotte Gray (1844-1925)
Mary Melissa Gray (1845-1933)
Harriet A Gray (1847-1924)
Joseph Gray (1849-1853)
Sarah Louisa Gray (1852-1860)

Sources:
1850 Census
1852 Find A Grave
1854 Marriage Record
1857 Minnesota Census
1860 Census
1870 Census
1880 Census
History of Washington County and the St. Croix Valley. 1881. Page 437.
1924 Death Record (Harriett Gray)
1925 Death Record (Angeline Gray)
1933 Death Record (Mary Melissa Gray)

Angeline Charlotte Gray (1844-1925)

Angeline Charlotte Gray (1844-1925) was born on February 26, 1844, in Brasher Falls, New York. Her obituary says she moved with her family to Lake County, Illinois in 1848 when she was 4. However, the 1850 Census lists her with her parents and younger sisters, Mary Melissa Gray and Harriet A Gray in Brasher, New York in Sept 1850.

Her mother died in 1852 and is buried in Diamond Lake Cemetery with a younger brother, named Joseph who was aged 4. Her youngest sister, Sarah Louisa Gray would eventually be adopted by the Peltons and pass away in 1860.

Angeline's father remarried in 1854 to Mary Gilder. Angeline would move around in the ensuing years. In 1856 she is listed in the Iowa census living in Alton, Iowa with Simon and Sarah Louisa Cramer, her aunt and uncle. Sarah is her mother's youngest sister. In 1857 she was in Minnesota with her father, step mother, her three younger sisters (Mary Melissa Gray, Harriet A Gray and Sarah Louisa Gray), and their half siblings, Jeanette and Theodore Gray. The 1860 census for her father does not list Angeline or her sisters living with him in Minnesota. We know by this time Sarah Louisa Gray has been adopted by the Peltons and died around August 1860. Census data for 1860 and 1870 for Angeline could not be located.

The 1870 census lists a farm hand named John Ridley living with the Peltons. Angeline married John Ridley on October 13th, 1869 in Lake County, Illinois. They moved to Emporia, Kansas where their two daughters were born. Angeline and her daughters are listed twice in the 1880 census. The first census shows her as "Sis" Ridley living with John, Edith and Nina. It was believed John died sometime in 1880 in Kansas. However, additional mentions of John Ridley have been found in Eureka newspapers. The Graphic newspaper on March 17, 1880 mentions that the J.W. Ridley family would be spending the summer in the East and that he would be staying behind. Later, in 1880, on a second census Angeline is listed as a niece to the head of household

Stephen and Elizabeth, living in Illinois with her two girls. There are additional mentions of J.W. Ridley and his business in the Greenwood County Democrat and the Graphic as late as 1883. To date no further mentions of Ridley have been found.

In the 1900 census Angeline is listed as a widow and works in washing with her daughters, Nina and Edith "Jennie" living with her. By 1910 she was living with her daughter, Edith, who is now married to James Holt Laycock with their adopted daughter Bernice. Angeline died on February 19, 1925. Her obituary shows her marriage to John Ridley on October 13, 1869 and states they moved to Emporia Kansas where they lived for 11 years until his death when she returned to Lake County. It lists her sister, Mary Melissa Gladstone (obit has typo with Gladson) residing in Kansas and her sister Harriet "Hattie" Roberts who died in Brownsville, Oregon two months previously.

Migration:
1844 Brasher Falls, New York
1851 Lake County, Illinois
1856 Alton, Iowa
1857 Baytown, Minnesota
1870 Emporia, Kansas
1880 Lake County, Illinois
1925 Lake County, Illinois

Children:
Edith "Jennie" (Ridley) Laycock (1878-1948)
Nina Ridley (1871-1940)

Sources:
1850 Census
1856 Iowa Census
1857 Minnesota Census
1869 Marriage Record

1875 Kansas Census
The Graphic - 7 Jan 1880 - Page 2
The Graphic - 17 Mar 1880 - Page 3
1880 Census, Illinois and KS
The Graphic - 30 Jun 1880 - Page 3
Greenwood County Democrat - 16 Aug 1883 - Page 2
1900 Census
1910 Census
1920 Census
1922 City Directory
"Obituary" - The Lake County Register, Libertyville, Illinois, 25 Feb 1925. Page 5
1925 Death Record
1925 Find A Grave

Mary Melissa Gray (1845-1933)

Mary Melissa Gray (1845-1933) was born on May 2, 1845, in Brasher Falls, New York. According to her sister, Angeline's obituary she moved with her family to Lake County, Illinois in 1848 when she was 3. However, the 1850 Census lists her with her parents and sisters, Mary Melissa Gray and Harriet A Gray in Brasher, New York.

Her mother died in 1852 and is buried in Diamond Lake Cemetery with a younger brother, named Joseph who is aged 4. Her youngest sister, Sarah Louisa Gray would eventually be adopted by the Peltons and pass away in 1860.

Mary Melissa's father remarried in 1854 to Mary Gilder. Mary Melissa would move around in the ensuing years. In the 1857 census she was in Minnesota with her father, step mother, her three sisters (Angeline Gray, Harriet A Gray and Sarah Louisa Gray), and their half siblings, Jeanette and Theodore Gray. The 1860 census for her father does not list Mary Melissa or any of her sisters living with him in Minnesota. We know by this time Sarah Louisa Gray has been adopted by the Peltons and died around August 1860. Census data for 1860 could not be located.

Mary Melissa married Eli Miller (1823-1874), on January 4, 1862 in Adel, Iowa. They would have six children together before Eli passed away in July 1874 in Madison, Kansas. Eli previously was married to Lucy Glenn and had five children from that marriage.

Mary Melissa married again on October 12, 1876 to Jacob Curtis in Greenwood, Kansas. They had two daughters together. Jacob married Martha Hall in 1854 and they had nine children together before she passed away in 1873. It is likely that the marriage ended in a divorce as it appears Jacob lived until 1903.

On December 15, 1884 Mary Melissa married Philander Bradbury Morse in Eureka, Kansas. They had one son together in 1886. Philander died in 1895.

Mary Melissa married one last time to Wesley Gladstone on May 30, 1912 in Kansas. That union would prove to be a short one, as Wesley died less than two years later on March 22, 1914. Mary lived to the age of almost 88 years, when she passed away on April 9, 1933 in Truro, Iowa. She had resided in Truro for the previous 18 years.

Migration:
1845 Brasher Falls, New York
1851 Lake County, Illinois
1856 Alton, Iowa
1857 Baytown, Minnesota
1862 Adel, Iowa
1870 Greenwood, Kansas
1920 Ohio, Iowa
1930 Truro, Iowa

Children:
(With Eli Miller)
Martha (Mattie) Jane Miller (1862–1946)

Paulinia Elinor Miller (1864–1883)
Harriet (Hattie) Angelina Miller (1866–1959)
Charles Henry Miller (1869–1955)
William Hairm Miller (1871–1956)
Mary Melissa Miller (1873–1950)
(with Jacob Curtis)
Grace Mabel "Gracie" Curtis (1878–1921)
Sarah Elizabeth Curtis (1880–1911)
(with Philander Morse)
Alphious Bradbury Morse (1886–1950)

Sources:
1850 Census
1856 Iowa Census
1857 Minnesota Census
1862 Marriage Record
1870 Census
1875 Kansas Census
1876 Marriage Record
1880 Census
1896 Marriage Record
1910 Census
1912 Marriage Announcement - The Eureka Herald and Greenwood County Republican - 30 May 1912 - Page 1
1920 Census
1925 Obituary - The Lake County Register, Libertyville, Illinois, 25 Feb 1925. Page 5
1930 Census
1933 Death Record
1933 Find A Grave

Harriet A Gray (1847-1924)

Harriet A Gray (1847-1924) was born on June 10, 1847, in Bombay, New York. According to her sister, Angeline's obituary she moved with her family to Lake County, Illinois in 1848 when she was a year old. However, the 1850 Census lists her with her parents and older sisters, Mary Melissa Gray and Harriet A Gray in Brasher, New York.

Her mother died in 1852 and is buried in Diamond Lake Cemetery with a younger brother, named Joseph who is aged 4. Her youngest sister, Sarah Louisa Gray would eventually be adopted by the Peltons and pass away in 1860.

Harriet's father remarried in 1854 to Mary Gilder. Harriet would move around in the ensuing years. In the 1856 Iowa census a 9 year old Harriet Gray was living with her uncle, Joseph Miles Soper and his family in Alton, Iowa. In the 1857 Minnesota census we found her with her father, step mother, her three sisters (Angeline Gray, Mary Melissa Gray and Sarah Louisa Gray), and their half siblings, Jeanette and Theodore Gray. The 1860 census for her father does not list Harriet or any of her sisters living with their father in Minnesota. We know by this time Sarah Louisa Gray has been adopted by the Peltons and died some time around August 1860. A 12 year old Harriet can be found on the 1860 census in Iowa back with her uncle, Joseph Miles Soper and his wife Angelina.

Harriet married Henry Martin Roberts (1841-1923) on October 16, 1864 in Hampton, Iowa. They would have eight children together. They lived in Iowa until at least 1885 before heading west to Oregon. Their youngest child, Edwin Earl Roberts was born in Crawfordsville, Oregon in 1889. Henry died in Brownsville, Oregon on October 15, 1923, and Harriet on August 7, 1824. They are buried in Brownsville Pioneer Cemetery.

Migration:
1847 Bombay, New York

1848 Lake County, Illinois
1856 Alton, Iowa
1860 Reeve, Iowa
1864 Hampton, Iowa
1880 Geneva, Iowa
1889 Crawfordsville, OR
1900 South Brownsville, OR
1924 South Brownsville, OR

Children:
Dora Isabella Roberts (1865–1930)
Charles Elmer Roberts (1867–1944)
Dewitt Clinton Roberts (1869–1936)
Glennie J W Schofield Roberts (1873–1872)
Evlyn Alfred Roberts (1876–1876)
Cyril Gray Roberts (1880–1945)
Luna Mable Roberts (1883–1953)
Edwin Earl Roberts (1889–1946)

Sources:
1850 Census
1856 Iowa Census
1857 Minnesota Census
1860 Census
1864 Iowa, Select Marriages Index, 1758-1996
1880 Census
1900 Census
1910 Census
1910, Civil War Pension Index: General Index to Pension Files, 1861-1934
1920 Census
1924 Death Record
1924 Find A Grave

Joseph Gray (1851-1855)

Joseph is not listed in any known census data. The only information we have on him is from his mother's gravestone where he is listed as age 4. The inference is that he was born after 1850 as he was not listed in the 1850 census in Brasher, New York and died young where he was buried with his mother, possibly after her reported death in 1852. Death records are not available for Mary Melissa or Joseph. Mary and Joseph's headstone was replaced at a later date. Compare their headstone to Sarah Louisa (Gray) Pelton's and that should be self-evident.

Source:
Find A Grave

Sarah Louisa Gray (1852-1860)

Sarah Louisa had a short life. She is not listed in the 1850 census when the Gray's were still living in Brasher and had not yet started their westward migration. She is listed as being born in Illinois in the 1857 Minnesota census and the 1860 census.

The 1857 Minnesota census we see Charles has brought his extended family together, if only for a short time. The 1857 Minnesota Census lists Angeline Gray, Mary Melissa Gray, Harriet Gray, and Sarah Gray with their half siblings, Jeanette and Theodore Gray. Charles 1860 census shows his daughters with Mary Melissa (Soper) Gray are no longer living in Minnesota with him.

By the 1860 census Sarah Louisa was living with her adopted parents Stephen and Elizabeth (Soper) Pelton. Also listed in the same census is her cousin, Jeremiah Conklin and adopted-brother George Pelton. It's believed she passed away some time after the July 20th date of the 1860 census and before October 1860 when her adopted father Stephen wrote his will as she is not mentioned in the will. The only child mentioned in the will is their other adopted child, George Pelton. No death records or obituaries have been found for Sarah Louisa Pelton so the events around her death are unknown.

According to Diamond Lake Cemetery records, Charles Gray bought four grave plots in 1852 after the death of his wife. She is in one of the plots with Joseph, Sarah Louisa (Gray) Pelton is in another one. The last two plots would not be used until the death of Robert Dallas Laycock in 1942 and Marvin Laycock in 1979.

After her death she is mentioned in the Lake County biographies of Stephen Pelton ("The Past and Present of Lake County Illinois" from 1877 and "The Portrait and Biographical Album of Lake County" from 1891) as their adopted daughter.

Migration:
1852 Lake County, Illinois
1857 MInnesota
1860 Lake County, Illinois

Sources:
1857 Minnesota Census
1860 Census
1860 Find A Grave
Past and Present of Lake County, 1877 - Page 409
Portrait and Biographical Album of Lake County, Illinois, 1891 - Page 643-644
Genealogy of the Pelton Family in America, 1892 - Page 252-253

Harriet Eveline Soper (1823-1890)

Harriet Eveline Soper (1823-1890) was born in Bombay, New York on April 9, 1823. She married Sylvester Smith Haskell (1823-1901) on December 5, 1843. They had ten children together. Her obituary states they moved west to Lake County, Illinois in 1849. Moving a year later to Two Rivers, Wisconsin to save money and build a home in DeKalb County, Illinois where they bought a farm. Sadly, the home burned down the day they were to move in. They lived in DeKalb County for many years before moving to Ord, Nebraska in 1876. Harriet passed away on May 9, 1891, and Sylvester passed away on February 28, 1901. They are buried together in Ord, Nebraska.

In May 1874 Orson Haskell, Orville Haskell and their brother-in-law A.M. Robbins purchased land from the Burlington and Missouri River Railroad Company and made their first plat of the proposed town. Later in the fall of 1876 their father Sylvester Haskell set up the first hotel, general store and post office. In 1879 Sylvester built a home in Ord. Ord was incorporated on June 23, 1881 with Sylvester serving on the first Board of Trustees. The Ord Weekly Quiz was founded by their son, William Haskell, on April 6, 1882. The Haskell family was instrumental in much of the early building of the town of Ord.

In addition to being industrious business owners, land owners, shopkeepers, running hotels, pioneers, soldiers, and more, almost all (sons and daughters) of Harriett and Sylvester's children have records of formal schooling.

A key resource to learn more about the Haskell family and their time in Ord, Nebraska, is the 1906 book "The Trail of the Loup". This book was written by Harold Foght (1870-1954) who was married to Alice Mabel Robbins (1878-1952), a grand-daughter of Harriet.

Migration:
1823 Bombay, New York
1830 Fort Covington, New York
1840 Brasher Falls, New York
1849 Lake County, Illinois
1850 Two Rivers, WI
1851 Paw Paw, Illinois
1876 Ord, Nebraska
1890 Ord, Nebraska

Children:

Orson Sylvester Haskell (1844 - 1921)
Orville Calvin Haskell (1846 - 1905)
Cynthia Celestia Haskell (1847 - 1928)
Alverdo Royal Haskell (1849 - 1937)
George W. Haskell (1851 - 1862)
Rosmond Imogene Haskell (1855 - 1936)
William Wesley Haskell (1857 - 1935)
Mary Elizabeth Haskell (1858 - 1955)
Emma Louise Haskell (1859 - 1863)
Elmer Elsworth Haskell (1862 - 1862)

Sources:
1870 Census
1880 Census
1884, Iowa, Marriage Records, 1880-1937
1885 Nebraska Census
"Mother Haskell Dead" - The Ord Quiz, 9 May 1890. Page 3
"Obituary" - The Ord Quiz, 28 Feb 1901. Page 5
The Trail of the Loup; being a history of the Loup River region by Foght, Harold Waldstein, 1906.

Orson Sylvester Haskell (1844 - 1921)

Orson Sylvestor Haskerll was born on December 7, 1844 in Brasher, New York. He moved with his family to Lake County, Illinois in 1849 then to Two Rivers, Wisconsin before settling in DeKalb County, Illinois where his family bought a farm.

Military records show he joined the 53rd Illinois Infantry Company D on November 18, 1861. He served 3 years, re-enlisting as a veteran. His company saw action in the following engagements: Battle of Shiloh (1862), Battle of Hatchie's Bridge (1862), Siege of Vicksburg (1863), Sherman's March to the Sea (1864), Carolinas campaign (1865), and

Battle of Bentonville (1865). He mustered out as a corporal in July 1865.

In 1866 the Illinois Soldiers' College was organized to enable disabled soldiers of Illinois regiments to continue their education. Col. Leander H. Potter was president, and remained in charge until 1873. The school name was changed to Northern Illinois College. Records for the Illinois Soldiers College show that Orson was conferred a Bachelor of Science degree on May 31, 1871.

He returned to Dekalb County and in the 1870 Census he is listed as living at home with his family. On July 7, 1872 he married Emma Goss (1851-1917) in DeKalb, Illinois. He later made a claim in Ord Nebraska in the summer of 1872 where he erected the first frame house in Valley County. His wife Emma was the first teacher in the upper half of the county. In May 1874 Orson Haskell, Orville Haskell and their brother-in-law A.M. Robbins purchased land from the Burlington and Missouri River Railroad Company and made their first plat of the proposed town.

In "The Trail of the Loop" Emma described an Indian scare in 1873 shortly after the Sioux Creek fight. Fearing an attack, several families hurriedly gathered at the Bailey homestead and spent a tense night waiting. Every man had a weapon. Water in all manner of containers was brought inside in case burning arrows were launched at the house. All the wagons were arranged in a semi-circle at the end of the house while they awaited the attack. She eventually fell asleep among the chaos until morning when no attack materialized they all returned to their homes.

Their daughter Lena Lenora Haskell (1877-1935) was born in Evanston, Illinois in 1877. By the 1880 census he was living in Boston with his family and is listed as a minister. His son, Chester Goss Haskell (1882-1950) was born near Chicago, Illinois in 1882 and by 1885 Orson and his family were back in Ord.

He was on the move again with his family and in 1900 he was living with his family and still listed as a minister in Liberty, Texas where he passed away on November 18, 1921. He is buried in the East Mount Cemetery in Greenville, Texas.

Returning to Lena Lenora Haskell, she married William Pierson (1871-1935) in Hunt, Texas on July 9, 1901. They had three children together, William Pierson (1902-1984), Alice Pierson (1907-1997), and Howard Pierson (1914-1994). William Pierson was a justice of the Supreme Court of Texas from January 1921 to April 1935.

William and his wife Lena were tragically murdered by their youngest son, Howard in April 1935. Howard reportedly suffered from mental illness for a long time. He was institutionalized until the 1960's when he was eventually released after being declared sane and found not guilty. During his institutionalization he escaped twice and was on the run for a significant time. After he was released, Howard moved to Spokane, Washington and lived until 1994. He legally changed his name to Robert T Hamilton. There are many contemporary accounts of the murder in the Austin American Statesman. Additionally there is a 2021 podcast, called Tenfold More Wicked "Murder in the Court" that dedicates several episodes to the case.

Irma Imogene Haskell (1891-1968) was born in Ord Nebraska in 1891. She attended the University of Texas in Austin. She was a school teacher in Goldpoint, Nevada when she met J.W. Dunfee where he was in the mining trade. From her passport application in 1921, Irma went to Hong Kong and Japan to serve as a teacher in the Philippine Service for 3 years and married J.W. upon her return. There is a ship manifest for the S.S. Golden State that departed from Hong Kong on December 10, 1921 and arrived in San Francisco on January 2, 1922. Her address is listed as Berekley, California. Note that Orson included his Civil War Pensioner No. 89225 on Irma's passport application.

In 1927 J.W. struck gold in Hornsilver, Nevada, later renamed Gold Point, Nevada. Prior to that, the area was known for its high grade silver ore, it was named Hornsilver. In 1928 J.W. and Irma adopted Camilla Hodgin and renamed her Nevada Imogene Dunfee (1926-2009). The Dunfee's built a home in Beverly Hills, California where Irma and

Nevada settled after J.W. passed away suddenly in 1931. More on the Dunfee's can be learned from the 2007 book by Alan Patera, "Hornsilver / Gold Point Nevada Silver turns to Gold".

Like many of the Haskell family, Joyce Juanita Haskell (1893–1982) was well educated. She attended the University of Texas in Austin. She moved around over the years. The 1930 census lists her as a laboratory technician at the Elgin State Hospital. It is unclear if she knew of her second cousin, Nina Ridley (1871-1940), who was a patient there or of any relationship with her family in nearby Lake County. It is also unclear how long she stayed there. By 1935 she was living in Ohio. She would return to Illinois and passed away in Evanston, Illinois in 1982. She is buried in East Mount Cemetery in Greenville, Texas.

Migration:
1844 Brasher, New York
1849 Lake County, Illinois
1850 Two Rivers, WI
1851 Paw Paw, Illinois
1877 Evanston, Illinois
1880 Boston, MA
1900 Liberty, TX
1921 Liberty, TX

Children:
Sylvester Merrit Haskell (1873–1874)
Eltie Evelyn Haskell (1876–1905)
Lena Lenora Haskell (1877–1935)
Chester Goss Haskell (1882–1950)
Viva Viola Haskell (1884–1949)
Bernice Beth Haskell (1888–1969)
Irma Imogene Haskell (1891–1968)
Joyce Juanita Haskell (1893–1982)

Sources:

1870 Census

Illinois, Marriage Index, 1860-1920

1880 Census

1900 Census

The Trail of the Loup; being a history of the Loup River region by Foght, Harold Waldstein, 1906.

1910 Census

1920 Census

Texas, U.S., Death Index, 1903-Index

U.S., Civil War Pension Index: General Index to Pension Files, 1861-1934

http://www.usgennet.org/usa/ne/topic/resources/OLLibrary/SCHofNE/pages/schn0340.htm

http://www.kancoll.org/books/andreas_ne/valley/valley-p1.html

https://en.wikipedia.org/wiki/William_Pierson_(judge)

https://www.nydailynews.com/true-crime-justice-story/ny-judge-pierson-murder-20220409-v4ltra663jeundhdwezhgthmlu-story.html

https://tenfoldmorewicked.com/season-three-episodes/

https://content.time.com/time/subscriber/article/0,33009,875387,00.html

U.S., Passport Applications, 1795-1925 (Irma, Orson)

Hornsilver / Gold Point Nevada Silver turns to Gold, by Alan H. Patera, 2007.

Tenfold More Wicked: Murder in the Court. Podcast, 2021. https://www.tenfoldmorewicked.com/

Civil War 53rd Illinois Infantry Regiment

https://civilwar.illinoisgenweb.org/r100/053-d-in.html

https://civilwar.illinoisgenweb.org/r100/053-i-in.html

https://en.wikipedia.org/wiki/53rd_Illinois_Infantry_Regiment

http://www.civilwararchive.com/Unreghst/unilinf5.htm#53rd

https://apps.ilsos.gov/isaveterans/civilMuster-Search.do?key=109860

Orville Calvin Haskell (1846 - 1905)

Orville Calvin Haskell was born on July 2, 1846 in Brasher, New York. He moved with his family to Lake County, Illinois in 1849 then to Two Rivers, Wisconsin before settling in DeKalb County, Illinois where his family bought a farm.

Military records show he joined the 53rd Illinois Infantry Company D on January 5, 1864. He was transferred from I Company. He mustered in a month later on February 9, 1864. His company saw action in the following engagements: Sherman's March to the Sea (1864), Carolinas campaign (1865), and Battle of Bentonville (1865). He mustered out in July 1865.

After the war he enrolled in the Jennings Seminary in DeKalb County, Illinois in 1872. No records could be found to indicate he graduated. He married Jeanette Lydia Winslow (1860-1936) in Polk, Iowa on June 26, 1884. In 1889 and 1890 city directories for Des Moines, Iowa show he was living at 744 W 17th and working in real estate.

In June 1894 he was admitted to the Leavenworth, Kansas Home for Disabled Volunteer Soldiers listed with a general disability. He remained there for six years when he was discharged in Oct 1900. He was listed as a widower in the record, which was incorrect as Jeanette died in 1936.

Orville died at a Salina, Kansas Hospital of cirrhosis of the liver on November 16, 1905. He was traveling through Kansas and had been in the hospital for several days. His son Burdette Haskell came to bring his body back to Ord for burial in the Ord Cemetery.

Migration:
1846 Brasher, New York
1849 Lake County, Illinois
1850 Two Rivers, WI
1851 Paw Paw, Illinois
1884 Polk, Iowa
1889 Des Moines, Iowa

1894 Leavenworth, KS
1905 Salina, KS

Children:
Burdette Winslow Haskell (1886–1913)
Earl Stanley Haskell (1886–1965)
Ruth Evelyn Haskell (1889–1987)
Rosamond M Haskell (1895–1963)

Sources:
1870 Census
1880 Census
Iowa, Marriage Records, 1880-1937
1889-1891 Des Moines Iowa, City Directory
U.S., National Homes for Disabled Volunteer Soldiers, 1866-1938
1900 Census
The Trail of the Loup; being a history of the Loup River region by Foght, Harold Waldstein, 1906.
1936 Find a Grave
Nebraska, U.S., Grand Army of the Republic, Burial Records, 1861-1948
http://www.usgennet.org/usa/ne/topic/resources/OLLibrary/SCHofNE/pages/schn0340.htm
http://www.kancoll.org/books/andreas_ne/valley/valley-p1.html
1936 Obituary. Chicago Tribune. Chicago, Illinois. March 22, 1936. Page 20.
Civil War - 53rd Illinois Infantry Regiment
https://civilwar.illinoisgenweb.org/r100/053-d-in.html
https://civilwar.illinoisgenweb.org/r100/053-i-in.html
https://en.wikipedia.org/wiki/53rd_Illinois_Infantry_Regiment
http://www.civilwararchive.com/Unreghst/unilinf5.htm#53rd
https://apps.ilsos.gov/isaveterans/civilMuster-Search.do?key=109874

https://apps.ilsos.gov/isaveterans/civilMuster-
Search.do?key=109875

Cynthia Celestia Haskell (1847 - 1928)

Cynthia Celestia Haskell was born on December 20, 1847 in Potsdam, New York. She moved with her family to Lake County, Illinois in 1849 then to Two Rivers, Wisconsin before settling in DeKalb County, Illinois where her family bought a farm. The 1870 census shows Cynthia living in DeKalb County with her parents.

The 1880 census shows her living in Sarpy County, Nebraska with her husband, Alphonse Marsh "A.M." Robbins (1849-1910) and family. The 1885 Nebraska census shows they were living in Ord, Nebraska and the The 1900 census shows them still living in Ord, Nebraska and that they were married in 1872.

A.M. Robbins was a successful attorney and was born in McHenry County, Illinois in 1849. Shortly thereafter his parents moved to Boone County, Illinois where he lived on a farm until the spring of 1866. He moved to DeKalb County and worked as a farm hand until the spring of 1868 when he enrolled in the East Paw Paw Classical Seminary & Teachers Institute. He graduated on July 4, 1873 with a Bachelor of Science degree. Cynthia is also a graduate of the East Paw Paw Classical Seminary & Teachers Institute.

After his graduation he studied law in the office of A.K. Truesdell in Dixon, Illinois and was admitted to practice law in the fall of 1875. He opened an office in Papillion, Nebraska on January 1, 1876. He practiced law there until moving to Ord in April 1881. A.M. passed away in Ord in 1910. Cynthia eventually settled in Lincoln, Nebraska where she passed away on Februaury 28, 1928. They are both buried in the Ord Cemetery.

Her daughter Alice Mabel Robbins (1878-1952) married Harold W. Foght, of Ord, Nebraska who wrote a history of Ord Nebraska called "The Trail of the Loop" in 1906. This book contains many of the details on the history of Ord and the Haskell and Robbins roles in founding the town.

Migration:
1847 Brasher, New York
1849 Lake County, Illinois
1850 Two Rivers, WI
1851 Paw Paw, Illinois
1880 Papillion, Nebraska
1881 Ord, Nebraska
1920 Lincoln, Nebraska
1928 Lincoln, Nebraska

Children:
Rose Imogene Robbins (1873–1960)
Edith Lucille Robbins (1874–1959)
Emma Eliza Robbins (1876–1965)
Alice Mabel Robbins (1878–1952)
Harold William Robbins (1883–1933)
Horace Alphonso Robbins (1883–1960)
Floyd Weston Robbins (1888–1950)

Sources:
1870 Census
1880 Census
1885 Nebraska Census
1900 Census
The Trail of the Loup; being a history of the Loup River region by Foght, Harold Waldstein, 1906.
1910 Census
1920 Census
1920, 1924, 1928 City Directory, Lincoln, Nebraska
U.S., Find a Grave Index

http://www.usgennet.org/usa/ne/topic/resources/OLLibrary/
SCHofNE/pages/schn0340.htm
http://www.kancoll.org/books/andreas_ne/valley/valley-p1.html

Alverdo Royal Haskell (1849 - 1937)

Alverdo Royal Haskell was born in Earlville, Illinois on November 4, 1849. The family may have stopped in Lake County before moving up to Two Rivers, Wisconsin. They then settled in DeKalb County, Illinois where his family bought a farm. The 1870 census shows Alverdo living in DeKalb County with his parents.

In married Emma Irene Mervine's (1851-1938) obituary it states she married Alverdo on December 25, 1873. She was born on February 25, 1851 in Paw Paw, Illinois, where she attended the East Paw Paw Classical Seminary & Teachers Institute and was a teacher for several years.

By 1890 Alverdo was listed as the postmaster in Hebron, Iowa. They would later be listed in the 1895 Iowa census and the 1900 census living in Grand River, Iowa. In 1903 he was listed in the Des Moines, Iowa City Directory. His obituary states that they settled in Howell County, Missouri in 1903 where he passed away on January 28, 1937. Emma died on October 19, 1938. They are buried in Evergreen Cemetery.

Migration:
1849 Earlville, Illinois
1850 Two Rivers, Wisconsin
1851 Paw Paw, Illinois
1890 Hebron, Iowa
1895 Grand River, Iowa
1903 Des Moines, Iowa
1903 Howell, Missouri
1937 Howell, Missouri

Children:

Vera Viola Haskell (1876–1970)

Ethel Eva Haskell (1884–1975)

Harriet Hope Haskell (1887–1975)

Walter Will Haskell (1890–1983)

Sources:

1870 Census

U.S., School Catalogs, 1765-1935, Jennings Seminary La Salle County, Illinois

U.S., Appointments of U. S. Postmasters, 1832-1971

1895 Iowa Census

1900 Census

1903 Des Moines City Directory

The Trail of the Loup; being a history of the Loup River region by Foght, Harold Waldstein, 1906.

1910 Census

1920 Census

1930 Census

1937 Missouri, U.S., Death Certificates, 1910-1969

Obituary, The Journal-Gazette, 28 Jan 1937

1937 Find a Grave

Obituary, The Journal-Gazette, 27 October 1938 Page 1.

Rosamond Imogene Haskell (1855 - 1936)

Rosamond Imogene Haskell was born on July 28, 1855 in DeKalb County, Illinois. She married John R. Williams on January 1, 1876 in Cook County, Illinois. They met at East Paw Paw Classical Seminary & Teachers Institute. They had two children together, Ruth Williams (1890–1987) and Rosalie Williams (1894–1976) Rosalie may have been adopted, Rosalie is listed as having been born in Czechoslovakia/ Bohemia.

They migrated with the family out to Ord, Nebraska and stayed there a number of years before moving to Lincoln, Nebraska sometime before 1920. John Williams passed on June 24, 1933, in Lincoln, Nebraska and Rose would pass a few years later on October 7, 1936. They are both buried in Lincoln Memorial Park.

Migration:
1855 Paw Paw, Illinois
1884 Ord, Nebraska
1913 Lincoln, Nebraska
1936 Lincoln, Nebraska

Children:
Ruth Williams (1890–1987)
Rosalie Williams (1894–1976)

Sources:
1870 Census
1880 Census
1885 Nebraska Census
1900 Census
The Trail of the Loup; being a history of the Loup River region by Foght, Harold Waldstein, 1906.
1910 Census
1920 Census
1930 Census
1933 Find a Grave
Obituary, The Lincoln Star, 30 Jun 1933, Page 4
Obituary, The Nebraska State Journal, 01 Nov 1936, Page 23

William Wesley Haskell (1857 - 1935)

William Wesley Haskell (1857 - 1935) was born on January 23, 1857 in DeKalb County, Illinois. He married Victoria Cecilia Cutler (1858-1950) on November 6, 1881 in Cook County, Illinois. The 1870 census shows William living in Paw Paw with his parents. In 1879 he was listed as attending the Northwestern University and Garrett Biblical Institute and living in Chicago. In 1880 the census lists him living on Michigan Avenue in Chicago and his occupation as a map publisher. He supported himself through college by selling maps. In 1881 he moved to Ord with his new wife after graduating from Northwestern University. By 1900 he was listed on the census as living in Ord Nebraska with his family and his occupation is listed as Editor Journal. In 1920 the census shows him living in Lincoln, Nebraska.

William co-published the Trail of the Loup book on the history of the area. It listed him as founding the Ord Weekly Quiz on April 6, 1882 as a Republican paper. He also established the Willow Springs Gazette in 1884 which later was sold to Jack Evans in 1887.

He died on August 16, 1935 in Lincoln, Nebraska after battling anemia for many years. He had received a number of transfusions over the last several months of his life. His wife Victoria had broken her hip shortly before his death and was not able to properly care for him. He was buried in the Ord Cemetery and Victoria was buried there in 1950.

The Lincoln Journal Star Lincoln, Nebraska, August 17, 1935 carried his obituary on the front page. He founded the Ord Quiz, shortly after his marriage to Victoria Cutler. He was known as a militant prohibitionist. His newspaper plant once had all the windows broken and another time the front of it was painted red. He sold the Quiz to H.D. Legget in 1918 before settling in Lincoln.

Migration:
1857 Paw Paw, Illinois
1881 Ord, Nebraska

1918 Lincoln, Nebraska
1935 Lincoln, Nebraska

Children:
Zilpha Leona Haskell (1883–1884)
Winifred Rose Haskell (1884–1976)
Costa Dell Haskell (1887–1970)
John Roscoe Haskell (1894–1986)
Zerna Mae Haskell (1898–1921)

Sources:
1870 Census
1880 Census
1885 Nebraska Census
1900 Census
The Trail of the Loup; being a history of the Loup River region by Foght, Harold Waldstein, 1906.
1910 Census
1920 Census
1930 Census
U.S., Find a Grave Index
Obituary, The Lincoln Star, 17 Aug 1935, Page 1
Obituary, The North Loup Loyalist, 23 Aug 1935, Page 1
Obituary, The Ord Quiz, 22 Aug 1935, Page 1

Mary Elizabeth Haskell (1858 - 1955)

Mary Elizabeth Haskell was born in LaSalle County, Illinois on April 17, 1858. She married Lewis Firkins in 1876. The 1870 census shows Mary living with her family in Paw Paw, Illinois. By the 1880 census she was living with Lewis Firkins and her daughter Vida R. Firkins in Wheeler, Nebraska. The 1900 census shows Mary living in Calhan,

Colorado with Vida and Willis Firkins. She is listed as a widower. However, some records indicate Lewis passed away in Florida in 1920.

Later on November 27, 1900 she married Henry R. Jones (1858-1936) in Colorado Springs, Colorado. The 1910 census lists Henry and Mary living in Colorado with Henry's daughter Ruth Jones (1892-?). By the 1950 census Mary is 91 years old and living with her son Willis in Fremont, Colorado. She passed away on May 17, 1955 and is buried in Lakeside Cemetery in Canon City, Colorado.

Migration:
1857 Paw Paw, Illinois
1880 Wheeler, Nebraska
1900 Calhan, Colorado
1955 Canon City, Colorado

Children:
Vida Rose Firkins (1878–1938)
Willis H Firkins (1880–1953)
Edith Pearl Firkins (1883–1942)

Sources:
1870 Census
1880 Census
1885 Nebraska Census
Colorado, County Marriage Records and State Index, 1862-2006
1900 Census
The Trail of the Loup; being a history of the Loup River region by Foght, Harold Waldstein, 1906.
1910 Census
1920 Census
1930 Census
1940 Census
1950 Census

1950 Find a Grave

Orange Phelps Soper (1827-1893)

Orange Phelps Soper (1827-1893) was born on March 11, 1827 in Bombay, New York. In the 1850 census it shows he was living with his father, mother and siblings, Clarissa Soper (1811-1832), Naomi (1813-1884), and Sarah Louisa Soper (1832-1909) in St. Lawrence County, New York. He married Hannah Gray (1835-1901) in New York in 1852. It should be noted that while his sister, Mary Melissa Soper married Charles Gray and his brother Joseph Miles Soper (1815-1891) married two Gray sisters, Abigail (Gray) Smith (1823-1880) and Angeline Gray (1820-1868) Hannah does not seem to be another Gray sibling.

On March 1, 1852, Orange Soper obtained a land patent for 40 acres under the April, 1820 Land Act in Buchanan County. This plot is just south of current day Fairbank, Iowa.

In 1856 he was living with his family and his mother Electa in Alton, Iowa. They live next to his sister Sarah Cramer and her family who have taken in their niece, Angeline Gray. Orange registered for the draft in 1863 and is listed in Fairbank, Iowa where he ultimately passed away on May 5, 1893.

There are two Orange Phelps Sopers, they are cousins to each other. Brothers Joseph Soper (1783-1851) and Remember Elijah Soper (1794-1872) both had sons named Orange Phelps Soper, who were named after Orange Phelps (1793-1885) who was their oldest sister, Elizabeth's son. Joseph's son, Orange Phelps Soper (1827-1893) was born in Bombay, New York and eventually settled in Iowa marrying Hannah Gray. Remember's son, Orange Phelps Soper (1828-1888) was born in Milton, Vermont and eventually settled in Watertown, South Dakota.

Migration:
1827 Bombay, New York

1840 Brasher Falls, New York

1850 Lawrence, New York

1854 Lake County, Illinois

1856 Alton, Iowa

1863 Fairbank, Iowa

1893 Fairbank, Iowa

Children:

Joseph Miles Soper (1853–1907)

Phoebe Caroline Soper (1856–1902)

Orange Alondon Soper (1858–)

Hannah Electa Soper (1862–1928)

Naomi Lovina Soper (1862–1932)

Charles Martin Soper (1864–1908)

Mary A Soper (1867–1930)

Julia Angeline Soper (1868–1908)

William O Soper (1870–1932)

Harriet Anna Soper (1878–1931)

Sources:

1850 Census

1852 - 1820 Land Act Wikipedia. https://en.wikipedia.org/wiki/Land_Act_of_1820

Land Patent Orange Soper 1 March 1852. Patent IA Vol 126, Document #12378. Retrieved from https://glorecords.blm.gov/search/

1856 Iowa Census

1860 Census

1863 U.S., Civil War Draft Registrations Records, 1863-1865

1870 Census

1880 Census

1881 "History of Buchanan County, Iowa". Cleveland, Williams brothers. 1881 Retrieved from https://archive.org/details/historyof-buchana00will/page/306/mode/2up - 15 Jan 2023

1893 Iowa, U.S., Wills and Probate Records, 1758-1997
1893 Find A Grave
1893 Iowa, Wills and Probate Records, 1758-1997

Joseph Miles Soper (1853–1907)

Joseph Miles Soper (1853–1907) was born in Buchanan County, Iowa in April 1853 where he lived his entire life. He married Elizabeth Amelia Cauch (1858-1890) on January 23, 1879. They had two children, Ethel Verona Soper (1880-1944) and Ellie Soper (1888-?). Elizabeth appears to have passed away by 1890 and Joseph remarried to Alice Berrier (1866-1900) on October 4, 1890. They had 3 children together, Lula Alice Soper (1892), Lena May Soper (1893-1925), and Joseph Allen Soper (1895-1969). Joseph is listed as a widower and a boarder in the 1900 census. He died on October 21, 1907 and is buried in Fairbank Cemetery.

Migration:
1853 Buchanan County, Iowa

Children:
With Elizabeth Cauch
Ethel Verona Soper (1880–1944)
Ellie Soper (1888–)
With Alice Berrier:
Lulu Alice Soper (1892–1965)
Lena May Soper (1893–1925)
Joseph Allen Soper (1895–1969)

Sources:
1856 Iowa Census
1860 Census
1870 Census

1880 Census

1880 Iowa, U.S., Births (series) 1880-1904, 1921-1944 and Delayed Births (series), 1856-1940 (Ethyl Soper birth record)

1890 Iowa, U.S., Marriage Records, 1880-1945

1892 Iowa, U.S., Births (series) 1880-1904, 1921-1944 and Delayed Births (series), 1856-1940 (Lulu Alice Soper birth record)

1900 Census

1905 Iowa State Census

1907 Find a Grave

1907 Iowa, Wills and Probate Records, 1758-1997

1925 Iowa, Death Records, 1920-1940 (Lena Soper)

Phoebe Caroline Soper (1856–1902)

Phoebe Caroline Soper (1856–1902) was born in Buchanan County, Iowa in April 1856 where she lived her entire life. She married John Mason Smith (1852-1937) on July 5, 1881. They had 6 children together, 5 of whom lived past infancy. She passed away on March 14, 1902 and is buried in Fairbank, Iowa in Fairbank Cemetery. John died in 1937 and is also buried in Fairbank Cemetery.

Migration:
Buchanan County, Iowa

Children:
Adda Leona Smith (1882–1974)
Arthur Ashford Smith (1883–1918)
Claude Orville Smith (1886–After 1937)
Earl Wallace Smith (1887–1951)
Leo M. Smith (1890–1920)
Orville J Smith (1893–1893)

Sources:

1856 Iowa Census
1860 Census
1870 Census
1880 Census
1881 Iowa, Marriage Records, 1880-1937
1895 Iowa Census
1900 Census
1902 Find A Grave
John Mason Smith Obituary, The Courier, Waterloo, Iowa, 17 Dec 1937, Page 26

Orange Alondon Soper (1858-1916)

Orange Alondon Soper (1858–1916) was born in Buchanan County, Iowa in 1858 where he lived his entire life. In the 1880 census his sister 14 year old Mary is listed as living with him and listed as his sister. The 1900 census he was listed living in a boarding house. By the 1910 census he was living with his brother Orville (head of the household), his sisters Anna, May and his brother Joseph Miles children with Alice Berrien, Lulu, Lena and Joseph (Allen). He never married and he passed away in 1916. His burial site is not currently known.

Migration:
Buchanan County, Iowa

Sources:
1860 Census
1870 Census
1880 Census
1885 Iowa Census
1900 Census
1905 Iowa Census
1910 Census

Iowa, Wills and Probate Records, 1758-1997

Electa Hannah Soper (1860–1928)

Electa Hannah Soper (1860–1928) was born in Buchanan County, Iowa in April 1860 where she lived her entire life. She married Eugene Chase (1866-1942) on November 15, 1900. They had 1 child together, Eugene had 3 girls from a previous marriage to Lucinda Ludwig. She passed away on September 7, 1928 and is buried in Fairbank, Iowa in Fairbank Cemetery. .

Migration:
Buchanan County, Iowa

Children:
Ernest Wesley Chase (1902-1975)

Sources:
1860 Census
1870 Census
1880 Census
Iowa, Marriage Records, 1880-1937
1895 Iowa Census
1900 Census
1910 Census
1920 Census
1925 Iowa Census
1928 Find A Grave

Naomi Lovina Soper (1862–1932)

Naomi Lovina Soper (1862–1932) was born in Buchanan County, Iowa on March 8, 1862, where she would live her entire life. She married

John Wesley Butler (1861-1941) in 1889. They had 6 children together. She passed away on September 17, 1932 and is buried in Rowley Cemetery in Rowley, Iowa.

Migration:
Buchanan County, Iowa

Children:
Charles Leroy Butler (1891–1943)
Gertrude May Butler (1892–1979)
Leta Belle Butler (1895–1971)
Guy Emerson Butler (1897–1972)
Anna E Butler (1898–1958)
Ethel L Butler(1904–?)

Sources:
1870 Census
1880 Census
1889 Iowa, Marriage Records, 1880-1937
1895 Iowa Census
1900 Census
1904 Iowa, U.S., Births (series) 1880-1904, 1921-1944 and Delayed Births (series), 1856-1940 (Ethel Leona Butler birth)
1905 Iowa Census
1910 Census
1920 Census
1925 Iowa Census
1932 Iowa, Death Records, 1920-1940
1932 Find A Grave
1945 Iowa, U.S., Births (series) 1880-1904, 1921-1944 and Delayed Births (series), 1856-1940 (1897 Guy Butler birth, affidavit by older brother Charles)

Charles Martin Soper (1864-1908)

Charles Martin Soper (1864–1908) was born in Buchanan County, Iowa in 1864 where he lived his entire life. In his will he lists his sisters, Anna Harriet Soper and Mary Abigail Soper, and his nephew Joseph Allan Soper as recipients of ⅓ of his estate. His brother Orange Alondon was listed as the executor of the estate. He never married and he passed away June 27, 1908 and is buried in Fairbank Cemetery.

Migration:
Buchanan County, Iowa

Sources:
1870 Census
1880 Census
1895 Iowa Census
1900 Census
1905 Iowa Census
1908 Iowa, Death Records, 1920-1940
1908 Iowa, Wills and Probate Records, 1758-1997

Mary Abigail Soper (1867-1930)

Mary A Soper (1867–1930), also known as Mae/May, was born in Buchanan County, Iowa in May 1867 where she lived her entire life. In the 1880 census 14 year old Mary is listed as living with older brother, Orange Alondon Soper. The 1920 census shows Mary (listed as May) living with her brother, Orville, and her youngest sister Anna. The 1930 census lists May and Anna as living in the Buchanan County Home as a boarder. She never married and she passed away on September 12, 1930. She is buried in Independence, Iowa.

Migration:

Buchanan County, Iowa

Sources:
1870 Census
1880 Census
1895 Iowa Census
1900 Census
1905 Iowa Census
1910 Census
1920 Census
1930 Census
Iowa, Death Records, 1920-1940
Obituary, The Courier, Waterloo, Iowa, 16 Sep 1930, Page 16

Julia Angeline Soper (1868–1908)

Julia Angeline Soper (1868–1908), was born in Buchanan County, Iowa on September 8, 1868. The 1900 census lists her as a servant for William Robinson in Fayette County, Iowa. She married Marcus Rogers on November 10, 1906. She died on November 3, 1908 in Oelwein, Iowa and is buried in Fairbank, Iowa.

Migration:
Buchanan County, Iowa
1900 Fayette County, Iowa

Sources:
1870 Census
1880 Census
1895 Iowa Census
1900 Census
1905 Iowa Census
1906 Iowa, Marriage Records, 1880-1937

1908 Find A Grave
1908 Iowa, Wills and Probate Records, 1758-1997

William Orville Soper (1870–1932)

William Oriville Soper (1870–1932) was born in Buchanan County, Iowa on December 28, 1870. By the 1920 Census he is listed as living in Independence, Iowa. By 1900 he was living with his brother Charles (listed as head of household, his mother Hannah, siblings, Electa, Mary (May), and Harriet (Anna). Also living with them are Joseph Miles children with Alice Berrien, Lulu, Lena, and Joseph Allen. The 1910 census is very similar, but Charles passed away in 1908 and Orville is now listed as head of the household. Additionally his brother Orange (Alondon) is living with them. In the 1920 census Orville was again listed as the head of the household and had his sisters, Anna and May, living with him and also a young cousin, named Alice. According to his obituary he had lived there for 20 years. He was listed as head of household by himself in the 1930 census. He never married and he passed away on September, 30, 1932 and is buried in Independence, Iowa.

Migration:
Buchanan County, Iowa
1920 Independence, Iowa

Sources:
1880 Census
1895 Iowa Census
1900 Census
1905 Iowa Census
1910 Census
1920 Census
1930 Census
1932 Iowa, Death Records, 1920-1940

Obituary, The Courier Waterloo, Iowa, October 3, 1932, Page 5.

Harriet Anna Soper (1878–1931)

Harriet Anna Soper (1878–1931), was born in Buchanan County, Iowa in 1878 where she lived her entire life. The 1880 census shows her living at home with her family. By 1900 she was living with her brother Charles (listed as head of household, her mother Hannah, siblings, Electa, Mary (May), Orville (William). Also living with them are Joseph Miles children with Alice Berrien, Lulu, Lena, and Joseph Allen. The 1910 census is very similar, but Charles passed away in 1908 and her brother Orville is now listed as head of the household. Additionally her brother Orange (Alondon) is living with them. In the 1920 census Orville, Anna, May were living together and had a young cousin, Alice living with them. The 1930 census lists May and Anna as living in the Buchanan County Home as a boarder. She never married and she passed away on July 29, 1931.

Migration:
Buchanan County, Iowa

Sources:
1870 Census
1880 Census
1895 Iowa Census
1900 Census
1905 Iowa Census
1910 Census
1920 Census
1925 Iowa Census
1930 Census
1931 Iowa, Death Records, 1920-1940

Elizabeth Charity Soper (1829-1904)

Elizabeth Charity Soper was born in New York on February 26, 1829. She married Stephen Edwin Pelton (1823-1891) on January 15th, 1850 in Lake County, Illinois. They are listed together on the 1850 census, along with her five year old niece, Angeline Conklin (1845-1880) from her sister Clarissa (Soper) Conklin. Clarissa's husband, Jeremiah Conklin, passed away a short time before.

Stephen's father, Stephen Edwin Pelton (1777-1827) passed away in 1827. His wife Susanna Eldridge (1786-1861) remarried in 1836 to Stephen's brother, Joshua Pelton (1779-1858). In 1843 he moved the family from New York to Lake County, Illinois. The Land Act of 1820 allowed for people to buy land in the West from the US Government. Joshua Pelton bought 72 and 72/100 acres of land in Lake County on March 10, 1843.

In the "Genealogy of the Pelton Family in America" it recounts that late in the summer of 1843, Stephen and his entire family came down with malaria. Within a three week span, Stephen's brother Joshua Pelton (1809-1843) and two of Joshua's children, Mary Jane Pelton (1833-1843) and Horace Pelton (1841-1843) passed away from the illness. They are listed as being buried in plot 36 in Diamond Lake Cemetery but to date there is no photo of any grave marker. This would likely make them some of the first people buried in Diamond Lake Cemetery.

The Peltons had no children of their own and over the years would take in many nieces and nephews. As far back as 1850 they took in Elizabeth's niece, Angeline after the death of her father Jeremiah Conklin. In 1853 they adopted George E. Pelton (1849-1918) and later adopted Elizabeth's niece, Sarah Louisa Gray (1852-1860). George was born in Ohio to as yet unknown parents. Sarah Louisa Gray (1852-1860) was a niece through Elizabeth's sister, Mary Melissa (Soper) Gray (1820-1852) who died young and is buried in Diamond Lake Cemetery. The 1860 census from July 1860 shows Stephen, Elizabeth, adopted children George and Sara Louisa and farm hand Jeremiah Conklin (1835-1905) living together. Jeremiah is Angeline Conklin's older brother and Elizabeth's nephew from her older sister Clarissa. Sarah Louisa Gray likely died around August 1860 and is buried in Diamond Lake Cemetery as Sarah Louisa Pelton. Stephen drafted a will in October 1860 and Sarah Louisa is not listed in the will, implying that she had already passed away and possibly was an impetus for Stephen to draft his will.

The 1870 census lists a newly married farm hand named John Ridley living with the Peltons. Elizabeth Charity's niece, Angeline (Gray) Ridley and older sister to adopted Sarah Louisa, married John Ridley in 1869. They moved to Emporia, Kansas where their two daughters were born. Later in 1880, Angeline and her daughters are listed twice in the 1880 census. The first census shows her as "Sis" Ridley living with John, Edith and Nina. According to Angeline's obituary John died sometime in 1880 in Kansas prompting his widowed wife and daughters to move back home to Lake County. We see later on in 1880, on the second census Angeline is listed as a niece to Stephen Pelton with her two girls and the Peltons. There is evidence that John Ridley may not have died in 1880.

A will and probate from 1892 shows Stephen prepared a will in October 1860, likely after the death of his adopted daughter Sarah Louisa. Stephen left $100 to his adopted son, George Pelton, and the rest to his wife. George would return to Libertyville from Kansas with his family after the death of his father in 1891 and in 1900 was living on Newberry Ave in Libertyville. The 1900 census shows Elizabeth also on Newberry Ave in Libertyville, living next door to her sister, Sarah (Soper) Cramer and Sarah's husband Simon.

A signature of "Mrs. E.C. Pelton" was found on a quilt of parishioners from Union Church done in 1889. This signature likely belongs to Elizabeth Charity. A copy of her signature can be found in the 1892 will and probate documents from Stephen's death and looks similar to what is shown on the quilt.

In 1895, a marriage record shows Elizabeth Pelton and Willard W Woodward were married in Lake County. There is an article in the Lake

County Independent from February 14, 1896, indicating Woodward had left because Pelton refused to feed his horse. Pelton was further upset because she could not receive his $6/month pension so she was seeking a divorce.

In 1903, the year before her death, Elizabeth had a notification in the Waukegan News Sun of her selling a plot of land in Libertyville to H.H Pegelow for $1,350. On April 8, 1904, Elizabeth died in Libertyville and is buried in Lakeside Cemetery.

A curious claim after Elizabeth's passing is found in the Waukegan News Sun on July 6, 1904. W.W. Woodward of Cleveland contested her will claiming their divorce was not a legal divorce and claims a dower interest of $2,000 out of her $5,000 estate. However, an article from August 5, 1904 indicates that Woodward's attorney later withdrew the case.

Migration:
1829 Bombay, New York
1830 Fort Covington, New York
1840 Brasher Falls, New York
1850 Lake County, Illinois
1904 Lake County, Illinois

Sources:
1850 Marriage Record
1850 Census
1860 Census
1860 - Illinois, Wills and Probate Records, 1772-1999 (Will)
1870 Census
Past and Present of Lake County, 1877 - Page 409
1880 Census
1892 - Illinois, Wills and Probate Records, 1772-1999 (Probate)
1895 Marriage Record
1900 Census

Portrait and Biographical Album of Lake County, Illinois, 1891 - Page 643-644

Genealogy of the Pelton Family in America, 1892 - Page 252-253

"Wants a Divorce" - Lake County Independent - 14 Feb 1896 - Page 1

"Real Estate Transfers" - Waukegan News-Sun - 9 Apr 1903 - Page 2

"EC Pelton Obituary" - Lake County Independent - 15 Apr 1904 - Page 5

"Claims Illegal Divorce" - Waukegan News-Sun - 6 Jul 1904 - Page 1

"Seeks Wife Estate" - Herald and Review - 8 Jul 1904 - Page 2

Quilt -

https://www.dailyherald.com/submitted/20180523/libertyville-mundelein-historical-society-announces-2018-summer-exhibit-and-open-house-season

https://shelflife.cooklib.org/2018/06/30/stitches-in-time-discovering-libertyville-history-through-the-1889-union-church-signature-quilt-part-1/

https://shelflife.cooklib.org/2018/08/04/stitches-in-time-discovering-libertyville-history-through-the-1889-union-church-signature-quilt-part-2/

https://shelflife.cooklib.org/2018/08/24/stitches-in-time-discovering-libertyville-history-through-the-1889-union-church-signature-quilt-part-3/

1820 Land Act Wikipedia. https://en.wikipedia.org/wiki/Land_Act_of_1820

Land Patent Joshua Pelton 10 March 1843. Patent IL Vol 88 pg. 257. Retrieved from https://glorecords.blm.gov/search/default.aspx

George E Pelton (1849-1918)

Multiple records list George Pelton as being born in Ohio to unknown parents sometime around 1849. In 1853 he was adopted by Stephen and Elizabeth Pelton. In the 1860 and 1870 census he is listed living with the Peltons. By 1880 he was living in Franklin Township in the northeast corner of Kansas and he was married on July 5, 1882 to Susan Mary Miller. They would have three children with two surviving into adulthood, Eva Pelton (1885-1948) and Edward Pelton (1885-1932).

George returned with his family to Libertyville, Illinois in 1891 after the death of his adopted father Stephen. The 1900 census shows George living with his family on Newberry Ave in Libertyville and he is employed as a teamster. According to a Lake County Independent and Waukegan Weekly Sun article in 1906 George saved the life of an unconscious Ben Clybourne who worked as a gas fitter for the North Shore Gas Company. Clybourne had entered a pit and succumbed to gas from a service pipe.

According to her obituary Susan passed away in 1910 as a result of spinal trouble. She was a member of the Mystic Workers benevolent society and a few weeks later George was paid out a $1,000 insurance policy. George lived until February 18, 1918, when he passed away at the home of his daughter Eva. He was also listed in his obituary as a member of the Mystic Workers who presided over his cemetery service. The Mystic Workers were essentially an insurance company that later became the Fidelity Life Association. They had a presence in Lake County during the early 1900's and can be found mentioned in various newspapers of the time.

Migration:
1849 Ohio
1853 Lake County, Illinois
1880 Franklin Township, Kansas
1891 Lake County, Illinois
1918 Lake County, Illinois

Children:
Eva Pelton (1885-1948)
Edward Pelton (1885-1932)

Sources:

1860 Census

1870 Census

1880 Census

1900 Census

Workman In Pit Overcome By Gas Lake County Independent and Waukegan Weekly Sun

16 Nov 1906, Fri, Page 5

1910 Census

Esteemed Citizen Passes Away Libertyville Independent, 21 Feb 1918, Thu, Page 1

1918 Illinois, Deaths and Stillbirths Index, 1916-1947

Sarah Louisa Gray (1852-1860)

See Mary Melissa Soper (1820-1852). Stephen and Elizabeth adopted Sarah after the death of her mother, Elizabeth's sister.

James P. Soper (1831-1872)

Not much information could be found on James P. Soper (1831-1872). He registered for the draft in July 1863 where he is listed as 33 years old and married.

Some records indicate he may have passed away in California in 1872. This is not confirmed.

Julia Jane Soper (1830-1884)

In 1849 Julia Jane Soper (1830-1884) married Edward Walston Jones (1819-1892) in Lake County. In the 1850 census they were listed living in Lake County with her niece, Clarissa (Soper) Conklin's daughter, 17 year old Ann Conklin. They are also listed as having a three month old child named Theron.

An 1870 census in California lists an Edward and Julia Jones with children Mary (17), and Edward (13). There is an additional child George (19) that is listed as born in England. Edward is listed as being born in Iowa in 1857 so the Jones appear to have been in Iowa for a time before continuing west to California. Edward Jones was registered as a voter in Yuba in 1867 and 1880.

By several accounts, but most notably described in the July 11, 1886 edition of the Los Angeles Times, stated that in 1882 Julia divorced Edward but allowed him to remain on their property. That would sadly end in her murder on December 4, 1884. Edward was tried but found not guilty of manslaughter.

He later tried to poison his son, Edward and his family and friends with rat poison in 1886. This led to him being found guilty of attempted murder and sent to San Quentin. Edward died in 1892 and is buried in Marysville Cemetery in Marysville, California. .

Migration:
1830 Bombay, New York
1849 Lake County, Illinois
1857 Floyd, Iowa
1867 Yuba, California
1870 Marysville, California

Children:
Mary Jones (1852-1916)
Edward Jones (1856-1908)

Sources:
1849 Marriage Record
1850 Census
1856 Birth in Iowa inferred from Census
1867 CA Voter Records
1870 Census

1880 CA Voter Records
Pomona Times-Courier, Dec 13, 1884 · Page 2
The Los Angeles Times, Jul 11, 1886 · Page 6
Los Angeles Herald, Jul 13, 1886 · Page 1
Los Angeles Herald, Jul 24, 1886 · Page 5
The Los Angeles Times, Jul 24, 1886 · Page 4
Los Angeles Herald, Jul 25, 1886 · Page 5
The Los Angeles Times, Jul 25, 1886 · Page 6
The Los Angeles Times, 19 Nov 1886 Pages 4-5
San Francisco Chronicle, Nov 23, 1886 · Page 8
San Francisco Chronicle, Nov 27, 1886 · Page 3
Marysville Evening Democrat, Mon, Apr 25, 1892
Marysville Evening Democrat, Mon, Apr 27, 1892
1892 Find A Grave

Mary Eva Jones (1852-1916)

Mary Eva Jones (1852-1916) was born in Illinois on December 6, 1852. The 1870 census shows her living with her parents in Marysville, California. By 1880 she was living with Charles Laney and her daughter Harriet Laney in Marysville, California. She married Charles around 1880 per the 1900 census and they were still living in Marysville. She passed away on November 7, 1916 from a cerebral hemorrhage. She is buried in the Yuba City Cemetery.

Migration:
1852 Lake County, Illinois
1857 Floyd, Iowa
1867 Yuba, California
1870 Marysville, California

Children:
Harriet Elizabeth Laney (1880–1960)

Eda Amelia Laney (1881–1901)
Francis Edward Laney (1884–1933)
Lulu A Laney (1888–1974)
Vera Laney (1890–1981)
Julia Teresa Laney (1896–1989)
Mabel C Laney (1897–)
Arthur P Laney (1898–)
John W Laney (1899–)

Sources:
1870 Census
1880 Census
1900 Census
1910 Census
1916 Find A Grave
Marysville Evening Democrat, November 10, 1916 Page 5.

Edward Jones (1856-1908)

Edward Jones (1856-1908) was born in Iowa on December 6, 1852. He married Florence McKenney in 1880. The 1870 census shows him living with his parents in Marysville, California. By 1880 he was living with his wife Florence in Yuba, California. In the 1900 census they were now living in San Diego, California. They had 3 children together. He passed away on May 1, 1908 and is buried in Mount Hope Cemetery in San Diego, California. Florence died on February 13, 1951 in San Diego, California and is buried next to Edward in Mt. Hope Cemetery.

Migration:
1857 Floyd, Iowa
1867 Yuba, California
1870 Marysville, California
1894 San Diego, California

1908 San Diego, California

Children:
Audrey M Jones (1882–1972)
Elta R Jones (1888–1978)
Roby Charles Jones (1892–1975)

Sources:
1870 Census
1880 Census
The Los Angeles Times, Jul 11, 1886 · Page 6
Los Angeles Herald, Jul 13, 1886 · Page 1
Los Angeles Herald, Jul 24, 1886 · Page 5
The Los Angeles Times, Jul 24, 1886 · Page 4
Los Angeles Herald, Jul 25, 1886 · Page 5
The Los Angeles Times, Jul 25, 1886 · Page 6
The Los Angeles Times, 19 Nov 1886 Pages 4-5
San Francisco Chronicle, Nov 23, 1886 · Page 8
San Francisco Chronicle, Nov 27, 1886 · Page 3
1900 Census
1908 Find A Grave
California, U.S., Death Index, 1905-1939

Sarah Louisa Soper (1832-1909)

Sarah Louisa Soper (1832-1909) was born on May 17, 1832 and is listed on the 1850 census in Brasher Falls, New York with her father, mother and siblings, Clarissa Soper (1811-1832), Naomi (1813-1884), and Orange P Soper (1827-1893). She married Simon Peter Cramer (1829-1908) on October 28, 1854 in Lake County. They had seven children together.

The 1856 Iowa Census lists Simon, Sarah and baby Mary living in Alton, Iowa. Her niece, Angeline Gray (1844-1925), is also listed as living with them. They lived next to her brother, Orange P Soper, and his family who have Electa (Mansfield) Soper (1790-1865) living with them. In the 1860, 1870, 1880 census they are still listed in Iowa. According to Sarah's 1909 obituary they moved to Nebraska in 1880. The 1885 Nebraska census shows Simon, Sarah and Birdie sharing a house with the Soloman Dalzell family in Sherman, Nebraska.

The 1900 census has them living next to her sister, Elizabeth Charity (Soper) Pelton in Libertyville on Newberry Ave. On November 17, 1908 Simon passed away in his home in Ewing, Nerbraska. A few short months later, his ailing wife went to Chicago to the home of her daughter Julia Cramer (1860-1942), where she passed away on February 2, 1909. She is buried next to her husband in Ewing, Nebraska.

Migration:
1832 Bombay, New York
1840 Brasher Falls, New York
1850 Brasher Falls, New York
1854 Lake County, Illinois
1856 Alton, Iowa
1870 Fairbank, Iowa
1880 Nebraska
1885 Sherman, Nebraska
1900 Libertyville, Illinois
1909 Chicago, Illinois

Children:
Mary Cramer (1856-1891)
Dewitt Cramer (1857-1919)
Simon Cramer (1858-1882)
Julia Cramer (1860-1942)
Elmer Cramer (1864-1883)
William Emile Cramer (1865-1935)
Birdie Cramer (1874-1910)

Sources:
War of 1812 Land Bounty Records - Joseph Soper
1850 Census
1854 Marriage Record
1856 Iowa Census
1860 Census
1870 Census
1880 Census
1885 Nebraska Census
1900 Census
1909 Find A Grave
"Death of Mrs. Cramer" - The Ewing Advocate - 12 Feb 1909 - Page 1

Mary Cramer (1856-1891)

Mary Cramer (1856-1891) was born in Iowa in 1856. She married Edwin B Rodgers (1853-1925) on December 13, 1874 in Iowa. They had one child, Alberta Rodgers (1876-1960) and the family later moved on to Nebraska. She and Edwin would divorce and Edwin remarried in 1888. Mary died Mary at the age of 34 years old on May 22, 1891 of an unspecified long term illness. She is buried in Ewing Cemetery in Ewing, Nebraska.

Migration:
1856 Alton, Iowa
1870 Fairbank, Iowa
1880 Nebraska
1885 Sherman, Nebraska

Children:
Alberta Rodgers (1876-?)

Sources:

1856 Iowa Census
1860 Census
1870 Census
Iowa, Select Marriages Index, 1758-1996
1880 Census
1885 Nebraska Census
1891 Find A Grave

Dewitt Cramer (1857-1919)

Dewitt L. Cramer (1858-1919) was born in Fairbank, Iowa on December 4, 1858. He married a Swedish woman named Christina Alice Anderson (1861-1904) on August 30, 1885 in Ewing Nebraska. They had three children together. Christina died in 1904 and Dewitt remarried on June 6, 1905, to Alma Walt Davis of Arkansas. Dewitt ran a general store in Ewing for many years. Dewitt died in Little Rock, Arkansas on September 24, 1919 and is buried in Lakeside Cemetery.

Migration:
1856 Alton, Iowa
1870 Fairbank, Iowa
1880 Sherman, Nebraska
1900 Chicago, Illinois
1905 St Anne, Illinois
1910 Chicagio, Illinois
1919 Little Rock, Arkansas

Children:
Arthur W. Cramer (1888-1919)
Christina Cramer (1891-?)
Alberta Cramer (1901-1904)

Sources:

1860 Census
1870 Census
Iowa, Select Marriages Index, 1758-1996
1880 Census
1885 Nebraska Census
1900 Census
1905 Marriage Announcement - The Commercial Appeal - 7 Jun 1905 - Page 7
1905 Arkansas, U.S., County Marriages Index, 1837-1957
1910 Census
1919 Find A Grave

Simon Cramer (1859-1882)

Simon Cramer (1859-1882) was born in Alton, Iowa on July 12, 1859. He never married and had no children. He died on June 20, 1882 in Ewing, Nebraska.

Migration:
1860 Alton, Iowa
1870 Fairbank, Iowa
1880 Sherman, Nebraska
1882 Ewing, Nebraska

Sources:
1860 Census
1870 Census
1882 Find A Grave

Susie Cramer (1860-?)

Susie Cramer (1860-?) was born in Alton, Iowa in 1860. No further records have been found, this could be Julia Cramer misnamed in the census form.

Migration:
1860 Alton, Iowa

Sources:
1860 Census

Julia Cramer (1860-1942)

Julia Cramer (1860-1942) was born in Fairbank, Iowa on February 12, 1860. She was a school teacher until she married Riley Howard (1857-1921) on July 22, 1879 in Blackhawk, Iowa. Riley was also a school teacher. They moved to Antelope County in April 1881 in an area that became known as Orchard. They moved to Dakota, Nebraska in 1913. They had six children together. Riley passed away in 1921 and Julia on February 28, 1942. They are buried in Orchard Hill Cemetery.

Migration:
1860 Fairbank, Iowa
1880 Jackson, Iowa
1881 Orchard, Nebraska
1913 Dakota, Nebraska
1940 Sioux City, Iowa
1942 Orchard, Nebraska

Children:
Harry Howard (1880–?)
Alma Howard (1881–1955)

Ira Riley Howard (1884–1969)
Wilber Howard (1885–1942)
Frank Howard (1887–1974)
Stephen Howard (1889–1960)

Sources:
1870 Census
1879 Iowa, Select Marriages Index, 1758-1996
1880 Census
1885 Nebraska Census
1900 Census
1910 Census
1920 Census
1930 Census
1940 Census
1940 U.S., City Directories, 1822-1995
1942 Find A Grave
1942 Obituary - The Eagle - 5 Mar 1942 - Page 1

Elmer Cramer (1864-1883)

Elmer Cramer (1864-1883) was born in Fairbank, Iowa on February 18,1864. He is listed in the 1870 and 1880 census living with his family. He died on January 20, 1883 and is buried in Ewing Cemetery.

Migration:
1870 Fairbank, Iowa
1880 Jackson, Iowa
1883 Ewing, Nebraska

Sources:
1870 Census
1880 Census

1883 Find A Grave

William Emile Cramer (1865-1935)

William Emile Cramer (1865-1935) was born in Independence, Iowa on June 4, 1865. He was married three times. The first to Mary Christina Decker in Racine, Wisconsin on December 22, 1885. They had one daughter together. They divorced and he married a second time to Zelda Madison Branch (1888-?) on January 4, 1910 in Chicago, Illinois. They divorced 7-8 years before his death. Shortly before his death he was married a third time to Ethel Allen in October 1934.

He received his undergraduate degree from the University of Nebraska and studied homeopathic medicine at the Hahnemann Medical College in Chicago graduating in 1888. He settled in the Kansas City area around 1895 and was the chair of surgery at Hahnemann Medical College.

After his graduation he studied homeopathy in the University of Berlin and in Vienna. He was made an American researcher for the University of Berlin and traveled between the US and Germany often. After one of these visits in 1931 he came home in ill health and eventually passed away on May 31, 1935.

Migration:
1865 Independence, Iowa
1870 Fairbank, Iowa
1885 Racine, WI
1895 Kansas City, MO

Children:
Frances M. Cramer (1889-1976)

Sources:
1870 Census

1879 Iowa, Select Marriages Index, 1758-1996

1880 Census

1885 Wisconsin, U.S., Marriage Records, 1820-2004

1888 Chicago, Illinois, U.S., Voter Registration

1900 Census

1910 Census

1910 Cook County, Illinois, Marriages Index, 1871-1920

1912 Virginia, U.S., Select Marriages, 1785-1940

1914 U.S. Passport Applications, 1795-1925

1920 Census

1922 U.S., Passport Applications, 1795-1925

1930 Census

1935 Missouri, U.S., Death Certificates, 1910-1969

1935 Find A Grave

1935 Obituary - The Kansas City Times Kansas City, Missouri 01 Jun 1935, Sat Page 10

1935 Obituary - The Lincoln Star - 2 Jun 1935 - Page 17

1935 Obituary - The Kansas City Times - 4 Jun 1935 - Page 6

1935 Obituary - The Kansas City Star - 2 Jun 1935 - Page 12

1935 Obituary - Des Moines Tribune - 1 Jun 1935 - Page 4

1935 Obituary - Chicago Tribune - 2 Jun 1935 - Page 22

1935 Obituary - The Ewing Advocate Ewing, Nebraska 14 Jun 1935, Fri • Page 5

1935 Obituary - The Nebraska State Journal Lincoln, Nebraska 02 Jun 1935, Sun • Page 17

Birdie Cramer (1874-1910)

Birdie Cramer (1874-1910) was born in Independence, Iowa on July 13, 1874. She was married to John Miller (1864-1934) on June 17, 1894. They had three children together in addition to a step-son and step-daughter from another marriage. Birdie died on February 6, 1910 in Chicago, Illinois and is buried in Ewing, Nebraska.

Migration:
1874 Iowa
1880 Fairbank, Iowa
1900 Chicago, Illinois
1910 Pearl, Illinois

Children:
Eulalia F. Miller (1898–1994)
Madeline Miller (1903–1977)
Mildred R Miller (1907–1999)

Sources:
1880 Census
1885 Nebraska Census
1894 Nebraska, Marriage Records, 1855-1908
1895 U.S., City Directories, 1822-1995
1900 Census
1910 Census
1910 Find A Grave
1910 Obituary - Chicago Tribune - 8 Feb 1910 - Page 18
1910 Probate Illinois, Wills and Probate Records, 1772-1999

Erastus Soper (1785-1857)

Erastus Soper (1785-1857)

Erastus Soper (1785-1857) was born in Poultney, Vermont on September 8, 1785. Erastus married Mary Martin (1788-1874) and had 13 children. Note that Mary Martin's brother, Isaiah Martin (1781-1859), married Erastus's sister, Charity Soper.

He lived in Milton, Vermont until 1840, where he is listed in the census in Bombay, New York and he died there on May 2, 1857. Erastus served in the War of 1812 in Dixon's Regiment Vermont as a private along with his brothers Joseph (1783-1851) and Remember Soper (1794-1841), nephew, Orange Phelps (1792-1885) and his brother in law, Isaiah Martin (1781-1859).

Migration:
1775 Poultney, Vermont
1787 Milton, Vermont
1840 Bombay, New York
1857 Bombay, New York

Children:
Elijah Soper (1807–1887)
Mary Elizabeth "Polly" Soper (1810–1903)
Elizabeth L. Soper (1812–1880)
Erastus Soper (1815–1899)
Melissa Soper (1817–1827)
Alonzo Soper (1819–1878)

Phoebe Soper (1820–1886)
Emily Soper (1820–)
Mehitable Soper (1821–1902)
Esther Soper (1823–1889)
Sally Soper (1824–1910)
Sabra O. Soper (1829–1850)
Orson Soper (1831–1921)

Sources:
1810 Census
War of 1812 Service Records
1820 Census
1830 Census
1840 Census
1850 Census
1857 Find A Grave
History of Chittenden County, Vermont. Syracuse, N.Y. : D. Mason & Co.1886.
1933 Johnson, Herbert T. State of Vermont Roster of Soldiers in the War of 1812-1814. The Messenger Press. Pg 395-396

Elijah Soper (1807–1887)

Elijah was born in Milton, Vermont in 1807. He married Mary Minerva Nay (1817-1898) in Vermont. Mary's maiden name is also mentioned in the Portrait and Biographical Album of Champaign County (1888). According to the 1850 and 1860 census they resided in Lake County, Illinois. By the 1870 and 1880 census they were living near Champaign, Illinois where he passed away on January 1, 1887. Elijah was buried in Elmwood Cemetery in Rantoul, Illinois and Mary is buried in Henry, Illinois.

The 1870 census shows Elijah and his family were living near his cousin/son-in-law, Milton H Soper (1836-1909) and Elijah's daughter Catherine Soper's (1845-1893) family. Catherine married her first cousin once removed, on January 18, 1862 in Waukegan, Illinois. Milton is the son of Remember Elijah Soper (1794-1872), who was a brother to Elijah's father Erastus.

Migration:
1807 Vermont
1850 Lake County, Illinois
1870 Champaign, Illinois
1887 Champaign, Illinois

Children:
Edwinna Soper (1843–)
Catherine A Soper (1845–1893)
Mary Elizabeth Soper (1856–?)

Sources:
U.S. and International Marriage Records, 1560-1900
1850 Census
1860 Census
1870 Census
1880 Census
1887 Find A Grave
Portrait and Biographical Album of Champaign County, Illinois, 1888. Page 878-879

Mary Elizabeth "Polly" Soper (1810–1903)

Mary was born in Milton, Vermont on January 23, 1810. It is believed she married James Madison Tabor (1807-1888) in 1833 in Milton but no marriage records have been located to date. Starting in the 1850 census, she lived in Swanton, Vermont with her family until her death on January 13, 1903. Her husband died in 1888 and they are buried in the Tabor Cemetery in West Swanton, Vermont. Her son, John Tabor's death record from 1932 verifies her maiden name of Soper.

Migration:
1807 Milton, Vermont
1850 Swanton, Vermont
1903 West Swanton, Vermont

Children:
Church Tabor (1835–1896)
Phebe Tabor (1837–1900)
Erastus Soper Tabor (1838–1921)
Elizabeth "Betsy" Tabor (1840–1892)
Mary Jane Tabor (1841–1841)
James Tabor (1842–1904)
John Adams Tabor (1846–1932)
Mary J Tabor (1846–1892)
Jane Lizzie "Jennie" Tabor (1848–1880)

Sources:
1850 Census
1860 Census
1870 Census
1880 Census
1900 Census
1903 U.S., Find a Grave Index, 1600s-Current
1903 Vermont, U.S., Vital Records, 1720-1908
1932 Vermont, U.S., Death Records, 1909-2008 (Son, John Tabor)

Elizabeth L. Soper (1812–1880)

Elizabeth was born in Milton, Vermont around 1812. She never married and by 1850 she was listed in the census living in a boarding house in Colchester, Vermont. On the 1870 census she was still in Colchester, Vermont and listed as working in a woolen mill. In 1880, she was living with her brother, Erastus, and her sisters Melissa and Sally in Bombay, New York. She passed away on September 28, 1880 and is buried in Hillside Rest Cemetery in Franklin County, New York.

Migration:
1812 Milton, Vermont
1850 Colchester, Vermont
1880 Bombay, New York

Sources:
1850 Census
1870 Census
1880 Census
1880 Find a Grave Index, 1600s-Current

Erastus Soper (1815–1899)

Erastus was born in Milton, Vermont in 1815. He was listed in the 1850 census in Bombay, New York living with his parents, Erastus Soper (1785-1857) and Mary Martin (1788-1874), and his sisters Mehitable Soper (1821-1902), Sally Soper (1824-1910), and brother Orson Soper (1831-1921). In the 1860 census he is listed with his mother Mary Martin (1788-1874) and siblings Melissa Soper (1817-?), Alonzo Soper (1819-1878), Sally Soper (1824-1910), and Orson Soper (1831-1921) along with various and nieces and nephews in Bombay, New York. In the 1880 census he is listed with his sisters Elizabeth L Soper (1812-1880), Melissa Soper (1817-?) and Sally Soper (1824-1910).

To further confuse the matter, there is another Erastus Soper born in 1815 but in New York, not Vermont. He married Lucinda Daggett in Ohio and lived in Ohio, Indiana and Alabama before also passing away in March 1899 in Alabama, and not New York. There are various sources online that confuse these two Erastus Sopers.

A careful read through of the 1850, 1860, 1880 census shows this Erastus was in Bombay, New York with the various siblings and parents listed here. Additionally there is a New York state census, and a New

York death record index listing that shows the Vermont born Erastus passing away on November 14, 1899.

Migration:
1815 Vermont
1850 Bombay, New York
1899 Bombay, New York

Sources:
1850 Census
1860 Census
1875 New York State Census
1880 Census
1899 New York, U.S., Death Index, 1852-1956

Melissa Soper (1817–?)

Melissa was born in 1817 in Milton Vermont. In the 1850 census she was living with the Almon family and her brother Alonzo Soper (1819-1878) in Bombay, New York. She is listed in the 1860 census with her mother, Mary Martin (1788-1874), siblings Erastus Soper (1815-1899), Alonzo Soper (1819-1878), Sally Soper (1824-1910), and Orson Soper (1831-1921) along with various nieces and nephews in Bombay, New York. No other references about her could be found.

Migration:
1817 Vermont
1850 Bombay, New York

Sources:
1850 Census
1860 Census

Alonzo Soper (1819–1878)

Alonzo was born in 1819 in Milton, Vermont. In the 1850 census he was living with the Almon family and his sister Melissa Soper (1817-?) in Bombay, New York. He is listed in the 1860 census with his mother, Mary Martin (1788-1874), siblings Erastus Soper (1815-1899), Melissa Soper (1817-?), Sally Soper (1824-1910), and Orson Soper (1831-1921) along with various nieces and nephews in Bombay, New York. There are no records of him marrying or having any children.

In the 1870 census he was living in Bombay, New York with his mother Mary Martin (1788-1874), siblings Emily M Soper (1820-?), Sally Ann Soper (1824-1910), Orson Soper (1831-1921), and niece Elezea A Sabin. In the 1875 New York census, he is still in Bombay, New York and is listed as the head of the household. He died on July 20, 1878 and is buried in Hillside Rest Cemetery.

Migration:
1819 Vermont
1850 Bombay, New York
1878 Bombay, New York

Sources:
1850 Census
1860 Census
1870 Census
1875 New York Census
1878 Find a Grave
1878 New York, U.S., Wills and Probate Records, 1659-1999

Emily Soper (1820–?)

Emily was born in 1820 in Milton, Vermont. In the 1850 census she was living with her parents in Bombay, New York. In 1860 she was living with By the 1870 census she was living with the her mother, Mary Martin (1788-1874), siblings Alonzo Soper (1819-1878), Sally Soper

(1824-1910), and Orson Soper (1831-1921) and a niece in Bombay, New York. There are no records of her marrying or having any children. No further records have been identified to indicate her death or where she may be buried.

Migration:
1820 Vermont
1850 Bombay, New York

Sources:
1850 Census
1870 Census

Mehitable Soper (1821–1902)

Mehitable was born in Milton, Vermont in 1821. In the 1850 census she was living with her parents in Bombay, New York. Some time between 1858 and 1860 she married John Rockhill (1822-1883) They are listed together living in Bombay, New York on the 1860 census. John was married previously to Moira Mott (1812-1858). From her gravestone Moira is buried in Hillside Rest Cemetery. She died on January 27, 1858 and the gravestone listed her as the wife of John Rockhill.

From the 1860 census the following children are listed: Amelia Rockhill (1846-1928), Charles Rockhill (1848-1942), Albert Rockhill (1850-1940), Eugene Rockhill (1853-1898), and Elijah Rockhill (1859-1890). Based on the death of Moira in 1858, all of these children are John and Moira's except Elijah who was born to John and Mehitable.

John passed away in 1883, it is unknown where he is buried. Mehitable was last seen in the 1900 census living with her niece Adda Pnemo in Bombay, New York. It is believed she died in 1902 but no records have been found to confirm that date.

Migration:

1821 Milton, Vermont
1850 Bombay, New York
1900 Bombay New York

Children:
John and Moira
Amelia Rockhill (1846-1928)
Charles Rockhill (1848-1942)
Albert Rockhill (1850-1940)
Eugene Rockhill (1853-1898)
John and Mehitable
Elijah Rockhill (1859-1898)

Sources:
1850 Census
1860 Census
1870 Census
1875 New York, U.S., State Census
1880 Census
1883 New York, U.S., Death Index, 1852-1956
1900 Census

Esther Soper (1823–1889)

Esther was born in Milton, Vermont in 1823. She married Hiram Comfort Sabin (1818-1883) and they had seven children together. Starting in the 1850 census she was living in Brashar, New York with her husband and children. Esther's older sister Emily Soper (1820-) is also living with them in Brashar. In the 1870 census and 1880 census they are still in Brashar, New York. Hiram passed away in 1883 and is buried in Flint Chaffee Cemetery. Esther died on February 12, 1889 but her burial location is unknown.

Her son Erastus S. Sabin (1850–1898) was found murdered near Tupper Lake with two gunshot wounds to the head. He was likely the victim of a robbery. Officials later offered a reward for finding the killers, to date it does not appear that they know who committed the murder.

Migration:
1823 Milton, Vermont
1850 Brashar, New York
1880 Brashar, New York
1889 St. Ragis Falls, New York

Children:
Eleazer A Sabin (1845–)
Augustus Sabin (1848–1905)
Julius Alvin Sabin (1849–1865)
Erastus S. Sabin (1850–1898)
Harvey Eugene Sabin (1852–1939)
Mary Sabin (1853–)
Martin Sabin (1858–1934)

Sources:
1850 Census
1870 Census
1880 Census
1889 New York, U.S., Death Index, 1852-1956
The New York Times - 29 Sep 1898 - Page 11
The Standard Union, Brooklyn, New York Thursday, September 29, 1898 Page 5
The Burlington Free Press, Burlington, Vermont · Wednesday, October 05, 1898 Page 2
News and Advertiser, Northfield, Vermont Tuesday, October 18, 1898 Page 7
The Chelsea Herald, Randolph, Vermont Thursday, October 20, 1898 Page 5

Herald and News, Randolph, Vermont Thursday, October 20, 1898 Page 5

1905 Oregon, U.S., State Deaths, 1864-1968 (Aurelius Sabin)

1934 Washington, U.S., Select Death Index, 1907-1960 (Martin Sabin)

1939 Oregon, U.S., State Deaths, 1864-1968 (Harvey Eugene Sabin)

Sarah "Sally" Soper (1824–1910)

Sarah was born in January 1823 in Milton, Vermont. In the 1850 census she was living with her sister Esther and her family in Brashar, New York. The 1860 census shows her living with her mother, Mary Martin (1788-1874), siblings Erastus Soper (1815-1899), Melissa Soper (1817-?), Alonzo Soper (1819–1878), and Orson Soper (1831-1921) along with various nieces and nephews.

By the 1870 census she was living with her mother, Mary Martin (1788-1874), siblings Alonzo Soper (1819-1878), Emily M Soper (1820-), and Orson Soper (1831-1921) and a niece in Bombay, New York. The 1880 census shows her living in Bombay, New York with her brother Erastus Soper (1815-1899), Elizabeth Soper (1812-1880), and Melissa Soper (1817-). Also listed are their nephew Augustus Sabin (1848–1905) and niece Melissa Nelson. Melissa is likely a daughter of Phoebe Soper (1820-1886). In 1900 Sarah is listed in the census living with her nephew, Augustus and his family.

There are no records of her marrying or having any children. New York State Death records indicate she died on March 23, 1910 in Bombay, New York. It is not known where she is buried.

Migration:

1823 Milton, Vermont

1850 Bombay, New York

1910 Bombay, New York

Sources:

1850 Census
1870 Census
1880 Census
1900 Census
1910 New York, U.S., Death Index, 1852-1956

Phoebe Soper (1827–1886)

Phoebe was born in Milton, Vermont in 1827. She married Philetus B. Nelson and they had six children together. Starting in the 1850 census she was living in Parishville, New York with her husband and oldest daughter Betsy. In the 1860 census they are still in Parishville and they have Betsy, James, Candance, and Sarah ("Sally") living with them. In the 1870 census they have Sarah, Roswell and Charlotte living with them in Parishville. By 1880 they only had Roswell at home with them. Phoebe died in September 1886 and is buried in Holmes Hill Cemetery and Philetus died in 1888 and is also buried in Holmes Hill Cemetery.

Migration:
1827 Bombay, New York
1850 Parishville, New York
1886 Parishville, New York

Children:
Elizabeth "Betsy" Nelson (1849–1930)
James Nelson (1851–1907)
Candance Nelson (1856–?)
Sarah "Sally" Nelson (1858–1938)
Roswell E. Nelson (1861–1914)
Charlotte M. Nelson (1863–1942)

Sources:
1850 Census
1860 Census

1870 Census

1880 Census

1913 New York, U.S., County Marriage Records, 1847-1849, 1907-1936 (Sarah E. Pritchard)

Sabra O. Soper (1829–1850)

Sabra was born around 1829 in Milton, Vermont. She is listed in the New York Mortality Schedules for 1850 which indicates she died on January 17, 1850 of smallpox. She has no records of being married or having any children. She is buried in Hillside Rest Cemetery.

Migration:

1829 Vermont

1850 Bombay, New York

Sources:

1850 New York, U.S., U.S. Census Mortality Schedules, 1850-1880

1850 U.S., Federal Census Mortality Schedules, 1850-1885

1850 Find a Grave

Orson V. Soper (1831–1921)

Orson was born in Milton Vermont in August 1831. He first appears in the 1850 census living with his parents in Bombay, New York. The 1860 census shows him living with his mother, Mary Martin (1788-1874), siblings Erastus Soper (1815-1899), Melissa Soper (1817-?), Alonzo Soper (1819–1878), and Sarah Soper (1824-1910) along with various nieces and nephews.

By the 1870 census he was living with his mother, Mary Martin (1788-1874), siblings Alonzo Soper (1819-1878), Emily M Soper (1820-), and Orson Soper (1831-1921) and a niece in Bombay, New York.

In 1880 he was married and living with his wife, Ellen Barrett (1842-?). He was still living in Bombay, New York with his family in the 1900 and the 1910 census. The 1915 New York census also lists him living in Bombay, New York. The New York Death Index lists him passing away on August 18, 1921 in Dickinson, New York. No records of where is buried have been located. His wife, Ellen is last mentioned in a 1928 obituary for their daughter, Anna.

Migration:
1831 Milton, Vermont
1850 Bombay, New York
1921 Dickenson, New York

Children:
Mina M. Soper (1882–1897)
Anna M Soper (1884–1928)

Sources:
1850 Census
1860 Census
1870 Census
1875 New York, U.S., State Census
1880 Census
1900 Census
1905 New York, U.S., State Census
1910 Census
1915 New York, U.S., State Census
1921 New York, U.S., Death Index, 1852-1956

Charity Soper (1789-1847)

Charity Soper was born in Milton VT, on May 1, 1789. She married Isaiah Martin (1781-1859) on Jan 25, 1806 in South Hero, Vermont. Charity Soper's brother, Erastus Soper (1785-1857), married Isaiah's sister, Mary Martin (1788-1874). Isaiah served as a sergeant in Captain Amasa Mansfield's (1769-1847) company in Colonel Luther Dixon's Regiment. Isaiah served with his brothers-in-law's, Joseph (1783-1851), Erastus (1785-1857) and Remember Soper (1794-1841) and nephew, Orange Phelps (1792-1885).

In 1854 Isaiah received a Bounty Land Claim under the September 28, 1850: ScripWarrant Act of 1850 (9 Stat. 520) for his War of 1812 service. Records provided from the United States Department of the Interior Bureau of Land Management General Land Office Records indicate he served in Captain Mansfield's company in the Vermont Militia in the War of 1812. He was granted 40 acres in Waushara County, Wisconsin on December 9, 1854 under Military Warrant Volume 850 pg 225, Document #54030. Note that this Document number is sequentially one more than the one assigned to Orange Phelps, Document #54029. The land was sold to Samuel Havenor for an undisclosed sum.

In 1860 Isaiah received the remaining 120 acres of his Bounty Land Claim this time under the March 3, 1855: ScripWarrant Act of 1855 (10 Stat. 701) for his War of 1812 service. Records provided from the United States Department of the Interior Bureau of Land Management General Land Office Records indicate he served in Captain Mansfield's company in the Vermont Militia in the War of 1812. He was granted

120 acres in Webster County, Iowa on April 10, 1860 under Military Warrant Volume 343 pg 164, Document #56384. The land was sold to Reuben Washburn for an undisclosed sum.

Charity and Isaiah had 8 children together. Charity died in Milton on March 20, 1847 and is buried in Miltonboro Cemetery. Isaiah died on April 21, 1859 in Milton and is also buried in Miltonboro Cemetery.

Migration:
1789 Milton, Vermont
1847 Milton, Vermont

Children:
Dexter B. Martin (1806-1845)
Richard Martin (1808-1887)
Elezer Martin (1811-1813)
Mariah Martin (1815-1841)
Isaiah Martin (1820-1885)
Nathan Martin (1822-1877)
Lucius C Martin (1827-1853)
Lira Martin (1831-1869)

Sources:
1789 Birth Record - Vermont, U.S., Vital Records, 1720-1908
1806 Marriage Record - Vermont, U.S., Vital Records, 1720-1908
1820 Census
1847 Death Record - Vermont, U.S., Vital Records, 1720-1908
1847 Find A Grave
Military Bounty Land Warrant Vol 343 pg 164. Document #56384. (120 Acres). April 10, 1860.
Military Bounty Land Warrant Vol 850 pg 225. Document #54030. (40 Acres) December 9, 1854.
Retrieved from https://glorecords.blm.gov/search/default.aspx

1933 Johnson, Herbert T. State of Vermont Roster of Soldiers in the War of 1812-1814. The Messenger Press. Pg 284

Dexter B. Martin (1806-1845)

Dexter was born on November 4, 1806 in South Hero, Vermont. He married Lura Elizabeth Cook (1822-1860) some time around 1840. Their son George Martin (1841-1862) was born in 1841. Dexter died on April 29, 1845 in Milton, Vermont and is buried in West Milton Cemetery. Lura remarried to Martin Ferris (1822-1897) some time around 1846, they can be seen in the 1850 census in Chazy, New York. George is listed as George Ferris on the census along with his half siblings, Eugene and Alice Ferris.

In his 1859 will Isaiah Martin (1781-1859) left $25 to his grandson, George Martin, son of his deceased son, Dexter Martin. Lura died on August 15, 1860 in New York and is buried in the West Milton Cemetery. In the 1860 census George is living with his uncle, Isaiah Martin (1820-1885) and his family in Milton, Vermont. On September 24, 1861 George enlisted in the Vermont 6th Regiment Company I and died in the Battle of Savage's Station in Henrico, Virginia on June 29, 1862. He is buried in an unmarked grave in the Seven Pines National Cemetery at Sandston, Virginia. He has a stone marker next to his mother Lura at West Milton Cemetery.

Migration:
1806 Milton, Vermont
1845 Milton, Vermont

Children:
George Martin (1841-1862)

Sources:
1845 Vermont, U.S., Vital Records, 1720-1908
1845 Find a Grave

1850 Census

Vermont, U.S., Wills and Probate Records, 1749-1999 (June 10 1859 Will, Isaiah Martin 1781-1859)

1860 Census

"Revised roster of Vermont volunteers and lists of Vermonters who served in the army and navy of the United States during the war of the rebellion, 1861-66" Montpelier, Press of the Watchman publishing co.1892. Pg. 209 https://archive.org/details/cu31924080774148/mode/2up

Richard Martin (1808-1887)

Richard was born on February 11, 1808 in Milton, Vermont. He is listed in the 1860 census as a carpenter living with William and Leonora Bean. He is still with the family in the 1880 census but is listed as a boarder. It is likely that the Beans are a shirttail relation as his dad's sister, Phoebe Soper married into the Bean family. Richard has no known marriage records or any known children. He died on February 3, 1887 and is buried in Miltonboro Cemetery.

Migration:
1808 Milton, Vermont
1887 Milton, Vermont

Sources:
1860 Census
1880 Census
1887 Find a Grave
1887 Vermont, U.S., Vital Records, 1720-1908
1887 Vermont, U.S., Wills and Probate Records, 1749-1999

Elezer Martin (1811-1813)

Elezer was born in 1811 and died on Halloween in 1813. He is buried in the South Hero Cemetery.

Migration:
1811 South Hero, Vermont
1813 South Hero, Vermont

Sources:
1813 Vermont, U.S., Vital Records, 1720-1908
1813 Find a Grave

Mariah Martin (1815-1841)

Mariah was born in Vermont in 1815. She married John Watson (1800-1861) and had two children. Mariah passed away on March 16, 1841 and is buried in Miltonboro Cemetery. Her gravestone lists her as Mariah P. Watson. Her death certificate from 1841 has her listed as Maud Watson. Her daughter Sarah's 1915 death certificate also lists her as Maud. John died in 1861 and is also buried in Miltonboro Cemetery.

Migration:
1815 Vermont
1841 Milton, Vermont

Children:
Sarah Watson (1836-1915)
Richard Watson (1838-1878)

Sources:
1841 Vermont, U.S., Vital Records, 1720-1908 (Mariah's death record)
1841 Find a Grave
1915 Vermont, U.S., Death Records, 1909-2008 (Sarah's death record)

Isaiah Martin (1820-1885)

Isaiah was born in Vermont in 1820. He married Paulina Lydia Smith (1835-1908) and had four children. He was listed living with his family in Milton, Vermont in the 1850, 1860, 1870, and 1880 census. He passed away on October 1, 1885 and is buried in Miltonboro Cemetery. His wife Paulina died in 1908 and is also buried in Miltonboro Cemetery.

Nettie's death record lists her mom's maiden name as Polina Green which is incorrect. Burr's death record from 1949 lists his mother as Paulina Smith. Pauline's 1908 death record and obituary both list her maiden name Pauline Smith.

Migration:
1820 Vermont
1850 Milton, Vermont
1885 Milton, Vermont

Children:
Aldes Martin (1857–1907)
Elmore Martin (1861–1878)
Nettie Sophia Martin (1866–1890)
Burr D Martin (1868–1949)

Sources:
1850 census
1860 census
1870 census
1880 census
1885 Vermont, U.S., Vital Records, 1720-1908
1885 Find a Grave
1890 Vermont, U.S., Vital Records, 1720-1908 (Nettie death record)
1908 Pauline Smith obituary. The Burlington Free Press, 13 Jan 1908 Page 6.

1908 Vermont, U.S., Vital Records, 1720-1908 (Pauline's death record)

1949 Vermont, U.S., Death Records, 1909-2008 (Burr's death record)

Nathan Martin (1822-1877)

Nathan was born in Vermont in 1822. In the 1850 census Nathan was living at home with his parents in Milton. He married Harriett Merrick around 1863 and they had three children. By the 1870 census he was married to Harriett and living in Milton with their daughter Agnes. Their middle child Jennie died young in 1868. Nathan died on April 8, 1877 and is buried in Miltonboro Cemetery. Harriett died in 1932 and is also buried in Miltonboro Cemetery.

Harriet's 1932 obituary lists her daughter, Agnes, living in Pasadena, California and Mrs. Myron Donaldson (Ella) living in Swanton, Vermont. Ella's death record lists her as a widow and her cause of death was suicide by drowning in Madison, New Hampshire in Silver Lake.

Migration:
1822 Vermont
1850 Milton, Vermont
1877 Milton, Vermont

Children:
Agnes Martin (1864–1946)
Jennie M Martin (1865–1868)
Ella M Martin (1871–1935)

Sources:
1850 census
1868 Vermont, U.S., Vital Records, 1720-1908 (Jennie death record)
1870 census

1877 Vermont, U.S., Vital Records, 1720-1908 (Nathan death record)

1877 Find a Grave

1895 Massachusetts, U.S., Marriage Records, 1840-1915

1932 Vermont, U.S., Death Records, 1909-2008

1932 The Burlington Free Press, 12 Apr 1932 Page 2 (Harriet obituary)

1935 New Hampshire, U.S., Death Records, 1650-1969 (Ella death record)

Lucius C Martin (1827-1853)

Lucious was born in Vermont in 1827. There are no records of him being married or having any children. Lucious died on June 14, 1853 and is buried in Miltonboro Cemetery.

Migration:

1827 Vermont

1853 Milton, Vermont

Sources:

1853 Vermont, U.S., Vital Records, 1720-1908

1853 Find a Grave

Lyra Martin (1831-1869)

Lyra Martin was born on July 18, 1831, in Vermont. It should be noted there are alternate spellings of her name, Lira/Laura/Lyra. Lyra is in the 1850 census (listed as Laura) living with her father, Isaiah living in Milton, Vermont. She married Ephraim Mills (1827-1893) and by the 1860 census she was living with Ephraim and her young family in Georgia, Vermont. She died in Georgia, Vermont on December 12, 1869 and is buried in Miltonboro Cemetery.

Lyra and Ephraim had twins in 1858, named Myron and Byron. It appears Myron died at a young age as no further records could be found after their birth record. Lyra is mentioned in her father's will filed in 1859. Isaiah Martin (1781-1859) left her $300.

Ephraim remarried in 1870 to Sarah Watson. They had two children together. Ephraim died in 1893 and is buried in Miltonboro Cemetery.

Migration:
1831 Milton, Vermont
1860 Georgia, Vermont
1869 Georgia, Vermont

Children:
Ephraim and Lyra
Lucius Chandler Martin (1854–1920)
Wilbur Prescot Martin (1856–1930)
Byron M Martin (1858–1916)
Myron Martin (1858–?)
Katie May Martin (1860–1937)
Fred E Martin (1862–1926)
Homer Jed Martin (1864–1940)
Ephraim and Sarah
Myrtle Maria Mills (1871-1921)
Richard Egbert Mills (1875-1943)

Sources:
1850 census
1858 Vermont, U.S., Vital Records, 1720-1908 (Byron and Myron's birth record)
1859 Vermont, U.S., Wills and Probate Records, 1749-1999 (Isaiah's will)
1860 census
1869 Vermont, U.S., Vital Records, 1720-1908 (Lyra's death record)
1869 Find a Grave
1869 U.S., Federal Census Mortality Schedules, 1850-1885

1870 Vermont, U.S., Vital Records, 1720-1908 (Ephraim and Sarah's marriage record)

1870 census

1880 census

1886 Iowa, Marriage Records, 1880-1937 (Wilbur's marriage record)

1916 Vermont, U.S., Death Records, 1909-2008 (Byron's death record)

Electa Lake Soper (1792-1869)

Electa Lake Soper (1792-1869)

Electa Soper was born in MIlton, Vermont on May 12, 1792. She married Amasa S. Mansfield (1792-1875) some time around 1815 and they had eight children together. Amasa was a veteran of the War of 1812. He served as a private and a teamster. Amasa served with his future brothers in law's, Joseph (1783-1851), Erastus (1785-1857) and Remember Soper (1794-1841) and Isaiah Martin (1781-1859).

In 1855 Amasa filed for a Bounty Land Claim under the Act of March 3, 1855 for his War of 1812 service. Records provided from the National Archives show Amasa initially filed in St. Lawrence County where he appeared before the Justice of the Peace, Nathan Rice, on May 18, 1855. He stated that he enlisted in Burlington, Vermont in September 1813 for a term of 3 months as a teamster under Captain John Johnson and commanded by General Hampton. Amasa only served for about 14 days before he was injured and received an honorable discharge from Colonel Thomas.

On July 31, 1856 the Third Auditor's Office in the Treasury Department identified that Amasa was paid in the receipt roll of teamsters attached to a detachment of 2,000 men under General Swarthout on the march from French Mills to Sacketts Harbor February 20 to March 31, 1814 which he was paid for 12 days at $8/day for a total of $96. There was another receipt roll for March 31, 1814 which he was paid for 9 days at $8/day for $72. Showing a combined 21 days of service and $168 paid out. For this, Amasa was awarded a Military Warrant for 160 acres under the Scrip Warrant Act of 1855 on April 1, 1861 in Anderson

County, Kansas. This property was signed over to William O'Keefe for an undisclosed sum of money.

Though born in Vermont by the 1850 census, Electa and Amasa were living in Brasher, New York. In the 1856 Iowa census they were found in Linton, Iowa in Allamakee County living near his brother Abijah Mansfield (1803-1867). This was short-lived as they were back in Brashar by the 1860 census.

In 1862 President Lincoln signed the Homestead Act into law after the southern states had seceded. The act allowed anyone over the age of 21 or the head of a household, with some restrictions, to apply for public federal land up to 160 acres. There were some requirements that the homesteaders had to reside on the land and do some basic upkeep and improvements to the property. According to the 1901 Michigan Pioneer and Historical Society Collections Volume 31 in 1863, while in their 70's, Amasa and Electa moved to Benzie County Michigan with a large colony of people (including the Fullers, the Pratts, the Conklins, and others) from St. Lawrence County, New York. These names stand out as a number of these families would inter-marry in Michigan after arriving in 1863 and these names are found elsewhere in the family lines here. Several members of the family filed under the Homestead Act for land patents.

In 1871 Amasa filed for a pension for his War of 1812 service. The records from the National Archives paint quite a picture of a bureaucratic nightmare. Starting in 1871 over the course of two years letters were sent back and forth to request the $8/month pension for Amasa. On May 21, 1871 he appeared in court and swore that he served "the full period of sixty days in the military service of the United States in the War of 1812". He states that he served three different times.

1. In September 1812 he served as a substitute for Isaiah Martin who was drafted in Milton, Vermont. He served in Captain Amasa Mansfield's Company under Colonel Luther Dixon. He stated that Captain Mansfield was his uncle. They were ordered to the

Canadian line and then ordered back to St Albans, Vermont and finally sent home with directions to stay ready for service. The draft was for a period of three months.

2. Enlisted in Captain John Johnson's Company at Burlington, Vermont in the latter part of June or early July, 1813 and was honorably discharged at Plattsburgh, New York three months later.

3. When the British came to Plattsburgh in 1814, he volunteered to drive a team away. He stated he was in a company under Captain Taylor who was detached by General McComb. During the battle several people in the company were killed or wounded. After the battle was over they were sent home without any formal paperwork.

This paperwork was affirmed by two witnesses, Sanford Fuller and Peter. W. McCrea. Sanford was Amasa's grandson and Peter his son-law, married to Mary Mansfield (1830-1910). This packet was sent to the Department of the Interior by the lawyer Amasa retained, George Griswold, and received on June 6, 1871.

On October 24, 1871 the Department of the Interior Pension Office requested the Third Auditor Office in the Treasury Depart furnish evidence of Amasda's enrollment, muster service and duty and assigned a claim number of 17777. The Third Auditor's Office received it on October 25, 1871.

The Third Auditor's Office responded on January 10, 1872 that they did not find any rolls for Captain Johnson's Company and that Amasa was not on the rolls for Captain Amasa's Company. They further stated that Amasa's name was not found on the rolls of either Captain James Taylor or Oliver Taylor's Companies.

The Pension Office sent a request to the Third Auditor's Office on January 12, 1872 to verify the enrollment, muster service or duty of Amsasa Mansfield serving as a substitute for Isaiah Franklin serving in Captain Amasa Mansfield's Company.

Amasa's attorney George Griswold sent a note on January 20, 1872 that he had forwarded a request for the depositions but had heard from them and gave it up and was trying to obtain the necessary proof elsewhere. In a note from the Third Auditor's Office on May 6th 1872, there was no evidence of Amasa Mansfield serving in Captain Amasa Mansfield's Company.

On May 13, 1872 the Pension Office sent a request to the Third Auditor's asking them to reexamine their records for any records relating to Isaiah Franklin serving in Captain Amasa Mansfield's Company and if there is any evidence to show that Amasa Mansfield served as his substitute. This is a very notable transcription error for Isaiah Martin. It is likely the Pension Office was referencing Franklin County. The Third Auditor's Office did not return any evidence.

There was a note from the Third Auditor's Office on May 23, 1872 stating there was no evidence of a Bounty Land application made by Amasa Mansfield. On June 29, 1872 the Third Auditor's Office replied that there was no evidence of an Isaiah Franklin serving in Captain Amasa Mansfield's Company.

At this point, the Pension Office must have realized the error in the Isaiah Franklin request. In a letter from the Pension Office dated July 6, 1872 they requested the Third Auditor's Office to furnish any evidence of Isaiah MARTIN enlisted in Captain Amasa Mansfield's Company. In an undated note, the Third Auditor replied that Isaiah Martin served September 25, through November 18, 1813.

On August 20, 1872 the Third Auditor's Office returned to the Pension Office that Isaiah Martin served as a sergeant in Captain Amasa's Company from Sept 25, 1813 to November 18, 1813. In another document from the Pension Office that is stamped August 23, 1872, there were a number of handwritten notes back and forth asking if George Griwswold is recognized as an attorney.

On December 7, 1872, Nathan Cook appeared before the court in Franklin County, New York. He stated that he is the same Nathan Cook in pension certificate No 3822 dated September 4, 1871. He served as a private in Captain John Johnson's Company in the Vermont militia. Cook testifies that Amasa enlisted into Captain John Johnson's Company for six months and served as a teamster in General Hampton's army in 1813 for a period of about 5 months and was honorably discharged at Plattsburgh. Cook further attests that he does not know the exact enlistment date or his discharge date but that he served as a private or teamster for more than 60 days.

On the same day, December 7, 1872, Orange Phelps appeared before the court in Franklin County, New York. He stated that he was drafted with Isaiah Martin and others into Captain Amasa Mansfield's Company in the town of Milton in the fall of 1812 for 3 months. He further states that Isaiah Martin hired Amasa Mansfield 2nd to take his place, as a substitute.

During the summer of 1813, Orange was a neighbor of Amasa Mansfield in Milton, Vermont. Orange knew that Amasa enlisted and was absent from his home farm. Orange knew that Amasa served in Captain John Johnson's Company during that time. He also stated that Amasa served in Captain Beeman's Company during the Battle of Plattsburgh in September 1814.

In a letter from George Griswold to the Court of Pensions dated December 16, 1872, Griswold stated that Amasa was old and had been in ill health. He was working to obtain the information and would forward it as soon as he obtained it. This letter was stamped by the Pension Office on December 23, 1872.

In another Third Auditor's note from January 27, 1873, based on Warrant No 43937 Amasa was credited for 21 days of service for February 20 to March 31, 1814 and another receipt for 9 days from March 31, 1814.

In a note from TD Yeager dated January 28, 1873 it states that 8 days of service under Captain Beeman from September 1814 during the Battle of Plattsburgh was allowed in the claim of Orange Phelps No. 16518 based on testimony of Amasa Mansfield and R.E. Soper.

In the final letter from the Pension Office dated January 30, 1873 Amasa's application was rejected. After a thorough review and much back and forth his claim as a substitute for Isaiah Marton was denied. Amasa's claim for service serving on Captain James or Oliver Taylor's Company was denied. Amasa was credited with service as a teamster In Capt. Conrad Saxe's Company and Capt. John Johnson's company for a total of 49 days, between February 20 to April 9, 1814. Further, counting the eight days from his service in Captain Beeman's Company during the Battle of Plattsburgh, that brings his total number of service to 56 days. Just short of the 60 needed to qualify for the $8/month pension.

Electa died in Almira on August 24, 1869 of consumption. After the death of his wife Amasa is living with his son, Amasa, in the 1870 census in Almira, Michigan. Looking at their neighbors, John Lake (husband of Maria Mansfield), Sarah (Mansfield) Fuller, Jeremiah Conklin are on the same page. Phebe (Mansfield) Pettis is on the next page, and Stephen Pratt, husband of Angeline Conklin, are on the previous page. Amasa died on May 18, 1875. They are both buried in West Almira Cemetery.

Migration:
1789 Milton, Vermont
1847 Milton, Vermont
1850 Brashar New York
1856 Linton, Iowa
1860 Brashar, New York
1863 Almira, Michigan
1869 Almira, Michigan

Children:
Phoebe Mansfield (1817-1880)
Sarah "Sally" Mansfield (1819-1874)
Charity Mansfield (1821-1897)
Amasa Sanford Mansfield (1824-1888)

Parmelia Mansfield (1826-1870)

Mary Mansfield (1830-1910)

Levia Mansfield (1832-1873)

Maria E Mansfield (1833-1897)

Sources:

1792 Birth Record - Vermont, U.S., Vital Records, 1720-1908

1850 Census

1856 Iowa Census

1860 Census

1861 Amasa Mansfield. Military Warrant. MW-0437-161. Document 43937. April 1, 1861. March 3, 1855: Scrip Warrant Act of 1855 (10 Stat. 701).

Retrieved from https://glorecords.blm.gov/search/default.aspx

1862 Homestead Act Wikipedia. https://en.wikipedia.org/wiki/Homestead_Acts

1869 Death Record - Michigan Death Records, 1867-1950

1869 Find A Grave

1870 Census

1901 Michigan Pioneer and Historical Society Collections Volume 31 pages 102-113

1933 Johnson, Herbert T. State of Vermont Roster of Soldiers in the War of 1812-1814. The Messenger Press. Pg. 280

War of 1812 Pension Application Files Index, 1812-1815

1933 Johnson, Herbert T. State of Vermont Roster of Soldiers in the War of 1812-1814. The Messenger Press. Pg 280.

Phoebe Mansfield (1817-1880)

Phoebe was born in Vermont in 1817. She married Reuben Pettis (1810-1863) sometime before the 1840 census. It is inferred that they were married and living together in Brashar, New York, at that time. The 1850 and 1860 census also lists them living in Brashar, New York.

In 1863 Reuben died and is believed to be buried in St. Lawrence County, New York.

In 1863 a widowed Phoebe Pettis moved with a large colony of people from St. Lawrence County to Benzie County, Michigan as recounted in the 1901 Michigan Pioneer and Historical Society Collections. She would later apply for land under the 1862 Homestead Act. She is listed with her family living in Almira, Michigan in the 1870 and 1880 census. She is believed to have died in Michigan in 1880, some time after the census was recorded. Her burial site is unknown.

Migration:
1817 Vermont
1850 Brasher, New York
1863 Almira, Michigan
1880 Almira, Michigan

Children:
Reuben Pettis (1842–)
Daniel Pettis (1844–1918)
Lucina Pettis (1845–1901)
Avelina Pettis (1846–)
Charles Ephraim Pettis (1849–1911)
Phebe Pettis (1856–1913)
Hannah Pettis (1857–1925)
Amasa M. Pettis (1858–1913)
John M. Pettis (1860–1937)

Sources:
1850 Census
1860 Census
1862 Homestead Act Wikipedia. https://en.wikipedia.org/wiki/Homestead_Acts

Land Patent Phebe Pettis. 1 May 1867. AGS-0241-189. Scrip #58. July 2, 1862: State Grant-Agri College (12 Stat. 503). May 20, 1862: Homestead EntryOriginal (12 Stat. 392)

Retrieved from https://glorecords.blm.gov/search/default.aspx

1870 Census

1880 Census

1901 Michigan Pioneer and Historical Society Collections Volume 31 pages 102-113

Sarah "Sally" Mansfield (1819-1874)

Sarah was born in Vermont in 1819. She married James M. Fuller (1806-1864) sometime before the 1840 census. It is inferred from the 1840 census and the age of their oldest children that they were married and living together in Brashar, New York, at that time. The 1850 and 1860 census also lists them living in Brashar, New York. In 1864 James died after moving to Michigan with his family. No records have been located to confirm this.

In 1863 Sarah and James moved with a large colony of people from St. Lawrence County to Benzie County, Michigan as recounted in the 1901 Michigan Pioneer and Historical Society Collections. Sarah would later apply for land under the 1862 Homestead Act. She is listed with her family living in Almira, Michigan in the 1870 census. She is believed to have died in Michigan on October 29, 1874 of consumption. Her burial location is not known.

Migration:

1819 Vermont

1840 Brashar, New York

1863 Almira, Michigan

1874 Almira, Michigan

Children:

John Wesley Fuller (1834–1895)

Melissa "Lizzie" Fuller (1837–1915)

Andrew Jack Fuller (1838–1890)

Ester Emily Fuller (1840–1884)

James Madison Fuller (1843–1881)

Joseph Fuller (1847–1850)

Emily Ester Fuller (1848–1924)

Mary Jane Fuller (1848–1917)

Electa Fuller (1851–1925)

Polly Fuller (1852–1919)

Nathan B Fuller (1853–1910)

Permelia M Fuller (1855–1934)

Emma Fuller (1857–1924)

Addie Evaline Fuller (1860–1930)

Sources:

1840 census

1850 census

1860 census

1862 Homestead Act Wikipedia. https://en.wikipedia.org/wiki/Homestead_Acts

Land Patent Sally Fuller. 1 November 1869. MI 247 Homestead Certificate 136, Application 283. May 20, 1862: Homestead EntryOriginal (12 Stat. 392)

Retrieved from https://glorecords.blm.gov/search/default.aspx

1870 census

1874 Michigan, U.S., Death Records, 1867-1952

Charity Mansfield (1821-1897)

Charity was born in Vermont in 1821. She married George W. Fuller (1822-1905). The 1850 and 1860 census also lists them living in Brashar, New York. In 1863 Charity and George moved with a large colony of people from St. Lawrence County to Benzie County, Michigan as recounted in the 1901 Michigan Pioneer and Historical

Society Collections. George applied for land under the Land Act of 1829. She is listed with her family living in Almira, Michigan in the 1870 and 1880 census. Her death record indicated she was married at the age of 18, and that she had 7 children, 4 of whom were still living at the time of her death on October 25, 1897. She is buried in the West Almira Cemetery. George died on June 2, 1905 and is also buried in the West Almira Cemetery.

Migration:
1821 Vermont
1850 Brashar, New York
1863 Almira, Michigan
1897 Alimira, Michigan

Children:
Sanford Amasa Fuller (1842–1913)
George W Fuller (1845–1867)
Mary Louisa Fuller (1845–1883)
William Rufus Fuller (1851–1914)
Lydia Elizabeth Fuller (1853–1936)
Cora Adaline Fuller (1856–1881)
Noah Elijah Fuller (1861–1907)

Sources:
https://en.wikipedia.org/wiki/Land_Act_of_1820
1850 Census
1860 Census
Land Patent George Fuller. 1 November 1864. MI 247 Certificate 2256, Application 272. April 24, 1820: Sale-Cash Entry (3 Stat. 566)
Retrieved from https://glorecords.blm.gov/search/default.aspx
1870 Census
1880 Census
1897 Michigan, U.S., Death Records, 1867-1952

1897 Find a Grave
1897 Charity Mansfield Obituary. Traverse City Record-Eagle. Traverse City, Michigan · Wednesday, October 27, 1897. Page 2.

Amasa Sanford Mansfield (1824-1888)

Amasa was born in New York in 1824. No records indicate he ever married. The 1850 and 1860 census listed him living in Brashar, New York. In 1863 Amasa moved with a large colony of people from St. Lawrence County to Benzie County, Michigan as recounted in the 1901 Michigan Pioneer and Historical Society Collections. He is listed with his father as a farmer living in Almira, Michigan in the 1870 census. The 1880 census listed Amasa as living alone and that he was either Maimed, Crippled, or Bedridden. His death record indicated he died in 1888 of St Vitus Dance, which is an autoimmune disease caused by rheumatic fever. His burial location is unknown.

Migration:
1824 New York
1850 Brashar, New York
1863 Almira, Michigan
1888 Almira, Michigan

Sources:
1850 Census
1860 Census
1870 Census
1880 Census
1888 Michigan, U.S., Death Records, 1867-1952

Parmelia Mansfield (1826-?)

Parmelia was born in New York in 1826. She is listed on the 1850 census in Brashar New York with her parents and sisters, Lydia (1828-?

), Mary (1830-1910), and Maria (1833-1897). There are no further confirmed records after 1850.

Migration:
1826 New York
1850 Brashar, New York

Sources:
1850 census

Lydia Mansfield (1828-)

Lydia was born in New York in 1826. She is listed on the 1850 census in Brashar New York with her parents and sisters, Parmelia (1826-?), Mary (1830-1910), and Maria (1833-1897). There are no further confirmed records after 1850.

Migration:
1826 New York
1850 Brashar, New York

Sources:
1850 census

Mary Mansfield (1830-1910)

Mary was born in New York in 1830. The 1850 census showed she was living with her family in Brashar, New York. In the 1860 census she is listed as living with her brother, Amasa and sister Maria in Brashar, New York next to their parents. In 1863 Mary and her family moved with a large colony of people from St. Lawrence County to Benzie County, Michigan as recounted in the 1901 Michigan Pioneer and Historical Society Collections.

Mary married Peter Wesley McCrea on September 22, 1866 in Grand Traverse Michigan. The 1880 census shows Mary and her family living in the mountains of Keene, New York where Peter's occupation was listed as a mountain guide. They later returned to Fife Lake, Michigan by the 1900 census, with Wesley and Lena living with them. Lena is listed at "Linsier" and has a listed birthdate of February 1875. This lines up with Lena's date of birth on her death record, February 2, 1875. Some family trees list Linsier and Lena as sisters. The 1900 census also lists Mary and Peter as being married for 34 years.

Mary died on July 2, 1910 and is buried in Fife Lake Cemetery. Peter died September 22, 1910 on what would have been his 44th wedding anniversary and is also buried in Fife Lake Cemetery.

Migration:
1830 New York
1850 Brashar, New York
1863 Almira, Michigan
1880 Keene, New York
1900 Fife Lake, Michigan
1910 Fife Lake, Michigan

Children:
Wesley A McCrea (1867–1944)
Lottie V. McCrea (1870–1901)
William W McCrea (1872–1915)
Lena M McCrea (1875–1931)

Sources:
1850 Census
1860 Census
1866 Michigan, U.S., County Marriage Records, 1822-1940
1880 Census
1900 Census
1910 Michigan, U.S., Death Records, 1867-1952
1910 Find a Grave

1931 Michigan, U.S., Death Records, 1867-1952 (Lena M McCrea)

Maria Elizabeth Mansfield (1833-1897)

Maria was born in New York in 1833. The 1850 census she was living with her family in Brashar, New York. In the 1860 census she is listed as living with her brother, Amasa and sister Mary in Brashar, New York next to their parents. In 1863 Maria and her family moved with a large colony of people from St. Lawrence County to Benzie County, Michigan as recounted in the 1901 Michigan Pioneer and Historical Society Collections.

Maria married John Horace Lake (1840-?) some time after the 1860 census. The 1870 and 1880 census shows Maria and her family living in Almira, Michigan.

Maria died on December 18, 1897 from cancer and is buried in Fife Lake Cemetery. John remarried in 1898 to Lucy Lewis (1855-1916) and passed away some time after that. The 1910 census shows Lucy as widowed.

Migration:
1830 New York
1850 Brashar, New York
1863 Almira, Michigan
1897 Fife Lake, Michigan

Children:
Sarah Eula Lake (1864-1953)

Sources:
1850 Census
1860 Census
1866 Land Patent John H. Lake. 6 February 1866. MI 240 Certificate 2277. April 24, 1820: Sale-Cash Entry (3 Stat. 566)
Retrieved from https://glorecords.blm.gov/search/default.aspx

https://en.wikipedia.org/wiki/Land_Act_of_1820

1869 Land Patent John H. Lake. 1 November 1869. MI 247 Homestead Certificate 139, Application 285. May 20, 1862: Homestead EntryOriginal (12 Stat. 392)

Retrieved from https://glorecords.blm.gov/search/default.aspx

1862 Homestead Act Wikipedia. https://en.wikipedia.org/wiki/Homestead_Acts

1870 Census

1880 Census

1897 Michigan, U.S., Death Records, 1867-1952

1897 Find a Grave

Remember Elijah Soper
(1794-1872)

Remember Elijah Soper (1794-1872)

Remember Elijah Soper (1794-1872) was born two years after the tragic drowning deaths of his brothers William and Elijah. He was likely named Remember Elijah after his brother, Elijah. He served in the War of 1812 as a private in the Vermont militia with his brothers Joseph (1783-1851) and Erastus (1785-1857) Soper, nephew, Orange Phelps (1792-1885), and brother in law Isaiah Martin (1781-1859). After the war, he married Permelia McNall (1801-1878) in Vermont in 1819. Note, the 1820 census shows Remember living with five others in Milton, Vermont including one female aged 16-25.

In 1853 Remember received a Bounty Land Claim under the September 28, 1850: ScripWarrant Act of 1850 (9 Stat. 520) for his War of 1812 service. Records provided from the United States Department of the Interior Bureau of Land Management General Land Office Records indicate he served in Captain Mansfield's company in the Vermont Militia in the War of 1812. He was granted 40 acres in Buchanan County, Iowa on August 1, 1853 under Military Warrant Volume 686 pg 404, Document #67316. The land was sold to his nephew, Joseph Miles Soper (1815-1891) for an undisclosed sum.

In 1860 Remember received the remaining 120 acres of his Bounty Land Claim this time under the March 3, 1855: ScripWarrant Act of 1855 (10 Stat. 701) for his War of 1812 service. Records provided from the United States Department of the Interior Bureau of Land Management General Land Office Records indicate he served in Captain

Mansfield's company in the Vermont Militia in the War of 1812. He was granted 120 acres in Blue Earth County, Minnesota on March 10, 1860 under Military Warrant Volume 134 pg 488, Document #67316. The land was sold to Abraham Grover and Truman Macneil for an undisclosed sum.

The "Portrait and Biographical Album of Lake County, Illinois" and the "Portrait and Biographical Album of Champaign County, Illinois" state that In 1847 he moved to Lake County outside of Waukegan, Illinois with his wife, Permelia, daughters, Adeline, Julia, Eveline, and Rachel, and two sons, Orange Phelps and Milton Hubbell. The 1850 census shows they settled in Benton Township.

In the 1860 census they were living in Vernon Township, Illinois. The "Portrait and Biographical Album of Champaign County, Illinois" says that in 1863 Remember Elijah, Permelia and Milton Hubbell returned to Vermont. However, the 1870 census shows Elijah and Parmelia living in Newport Township, Illinois. In the "Portrait and Biographical Album of Lake County, Illinois" his daughter Adeline related that Remember and Permilila visited Illinois several times so it is possible they kept a residence in Illinois or were counted there by the census taker.

Remember appeared in Franklin County court on November 9, 1872 to testify that Orange Phelps (1792-1885) served with him in Captain Beeman's Company in September of 1814 at the Battle of Plattsburgh. He died shortly after that on November 24, 1872. Permelia passed away in 1878 in Johnson, Vermont. Both are buried in Miltonboro Cemetery.

Migration:
1794 Milton, Vermont
1847 Lake County, Illinois
1863 Fairfax, Vermont
1872 Fairfax, Vermont

Children:
Adeline Soper (1820–1903)
Harriet Soper (1820–1820)
Julia Soper (1824–1898)
Amasa Soper (1826–1827)
Orange Phelps Soper (1827–1888)
Eveline Soper (1830–1895)
Rachel Soper (1833–1899)
Milton Hubble Soper (1836–1909)

Sources:
1794 Birth Record - Vermont, U.S., Vital Records, 1720-1908
1812 - U.S., War of 1812 Service Records, 1812-1815
1820 Census
1850 Census
1853 Military Warrant MW-0686-404. Document 61242. August 1, 1853: September 28, 1850: ScripWarrant Act of 1850 (9 Stat. 520)
1860 Military Warrant MW-134-488, Document 67316. March 10, 1860: March 3, 1855: ScripWarrant Act of 1855 (10 Stat. 701)
Retrieved from https://glorecords.blm.gov/search/default.asp
1860 Census
1870 Census
1872 Death Record - Vermont, U.S., Vital Records, 1720-1908
1872 Find A Grave
1873 Probate Records - Vermont, U.S., Wills and Probate Records, 1749-1999
Portrait and Biographical Album of Lake County, Illinois, 1891. Page 535-536
Portrait and Biographical Album of Champaign County, Illinois, 1888. Page 878-879
1933 Johnson, Herbert T. State of Vermont Roster of Soldiers in the War of 1812-1814. The Messenger Press. Pg 395-396

"Tombstone Tuesday: Remember Elijah Soper" - https://digging-history.com/2015/01/27/tombstone-tuesday-remember-elijah-soper/ retrieved 1 Jan 2022.

Harriet Soper (1820–1820)

It is believed Harriet was born in 1820. The 1820 census in Milton with her father listed on it, shows 2 free white persons under 16 living there. The only other document concerning Harriet is a death record showing her date of death on November 16, 1820 and that she is buried in Milton Plains.

Migration:
1820 Milton, Vermont

Sources:
1820 Vermont, U.S., Vital Records, 1720-1908

Adeline Soper (1821–1903)

Adeline was born on December 9, 1821, in Vermont. She came to Lake County, Illinois with her family in 1847 and on April 3, 1848 Adeline married Elijah Fink Willis (E.F.W.) Eddy (1821-1902) in Lake County. According to "Portrait and Biographical Album of Lake County" which has a profile on E. F. W., they were early homesteaders in Lake County. She went to work as a school teacher and E. F. W. worked as a farmer. It was noted in her obituary that Adeline had lost her sight for the last 20 years of her life. E.F.W. passed away on July 2, 1902, and Adeline passed away on January 6, 1903, and they are buried in Greenwood Cemetery.

Migration:
1821 Vermont
1847 Lake County, Illinois
1903 Lake County, Illinois

Children:
Leando M. Eddy (1849–1926)
Permillia "Millie" Ann Eddy (1850–1903)
Celeste J Eddy (1856–1944)
Remember E. Eddy (1859–1903)
Sarah E Eddy (1864–1932)
Ada E. Eddy (1866–1943)

Sources:
1850 census
1860 census
1870 census
1880 census
1900 census
1848 Marriage Record
Portrait and Biographical Album of Lake County, Illinois, 1891.
Page 535-536
Waukegan News-Sun, Waukegan, Illinois · Monday, July 14, 1902
Obituary - Lake County Independent - 9 Jan 1903 - Page 1
1903 Find a Grave

Julia Soper (1824–1898)

Julia was born in Vermont on February 8, 1824. In the 1850 census Julia was married to Martin Hawley (1812-1892) and living in Sheboygan Falls, Wisconsin with their son J.U. (1846-), Orange Buck (1827-1917) and her sister Rachel Soper (1833-1899). Orange and Rachel would later be married in Lake County, Illinois in 1852. In the 1860 census, Julia and Martin are still living in Sheboygan Falls, Wisconsin with their 8 year old daughter Choloe. J.U. is no longer listed with the family and there are no further records of him at this time. By the 1870 census Julia and Martin returned to Vermont with Chloe.

Martin passed away in 1892 and Julia passed away October 26, 1898 both are buried in Carroll Hill Cemetery in Fairfax, Vermont.

Migration:
1824 Vermont
1847 Lake County, Illinois
1850 Sheboygan Falls, Wisconsin
1870 Fairfax, Vermont
1898 Fairfax, Vermont

Children:
J U Hawley (1846–)
Chloe P Hawley (1851–1931)

Sources:
1850 census
1860 census
1870 census
1880 census
Portrait and Biographical Album of Champaign County, Illinois, 1888. Page 878-879
1892 Vermont, U.S., Wills and Probate Records, 1749-1999
1898 Find a Grave

Amasa Soper (1826–1827)

Amasa was born in 1826 and died on April 8, 1827 at age 14 months. The only known record of Amasa is his grave marker at the Miltonboro Cemetery. The marker reads "In memory of Amasa Son of Remember & Permilia Soper who died Apr 8th, 1827 E. 14 months".

Migration:
1826 Milton, Vermont
1827 Milton, Vermont

Sources:
1827 Find a Grave

Orange Phelps Soper (1828–1888)

Orange was born in Milton, Vermont on April 5, 1828. He married Jerusha Ables on May 13, 1850 in Vermont and in the 1850 census they are living with his parents in Lake County, Illinois. In the 1860 census he is living in Lima, Wisconsin (near Sheboygan Falls) with Jerusha and his children. In 1863 Orange was drafted into the Vermont militia in Lamoille, Vermont. Jerusha died on December 16, 1865 in Greensboro, Vermont from consumption.

Orange remarried in 1866 to Laura Harrington (1845-?). Laura is listed in the 1860 census, living with the Lawton family in Fairfax, Virginia. The 1880 census shows Orange and his family with Laura living together in Middlefork, Illinois. Orange passed away on February 29, 1888 in Watertown, South Dakota where he was buried in Mt. Hope Cemetery.

There are two Orange Phelps Sopers who are cousins to each other. The brothers, Joseph Soper (1783-1851) and Remember Elijah Soper (1794-1872) both had sons named Orange Phelps Soper, likely named after Orange Phelps (1793-1885) who was the only son of their older sister, Elizabeth. Joseph's son, Orange Phelps Soper (1827-1893) was born in Bombay, New York and eventually settled in Iowa marrying Hannah Gray. Remember's son, Orange Phelps Soper (1828-1888), was born in Milton, Vermont and eventually died in Watertown, South Dakota.

From the "Portrait and Biographical Album of Champaign County, Illinois" Orange and his brother engaged in some land speculation in southwest Missouri and Harwood Township, Illinois on land purchased from the Illinois Central Railroad Company during the 1860's. Eventually in 1868 Milton set roots there with his family where he established a farm.

Posted on Ancestry, "A Simple Story of Life and Love on the Dakota Plains" by John Manning Stewart from 2006 contains a rather remarkable series of letters from Helen Thurnau to Phoebe Laura Kennedy, Orange's granddaughter written in the 1930's. Orange's daughter, Laura Idella Soper (1872–1893) married John Henry Kennedy (1863-1919) and Laura died young after their son Harold was born in 1893. During this difficult time, John was reluctantly forced to give up his children, Phoebe and Harold, for adoption to the Cartford family. John later remarried to Helen Thurnau (1875-1960) in 1895. Helen wrote a number of letters to John and Laura Idella's daughter, Phoebe, sharing what Helen knew of their family history and the regret her father John had for giving them up.

Migration:
1828 Milton, Vermont
1850 Lake County, Illinois
1860 Lima, Wisconsin
1865 Greeenboro, Vermont
1866 Johnson, Vermont
1880 Middlefork, Illinois
1888 Watertown, South Dakota

Children:
With Jerusha
Emogene Jerusha Soper (1851–1929)
Hubbell Soper (1853–1917)
With Laura
Louella Soper (1871–)
Laura Idella Soper (1872–1893)
Elbert Wesley Soper (1875–1920)
Katherine Soper (1878–)

Sources:

1850 census

1850 Vermont, U.S., Vital Records, 1720-1908

1860 census

1865 Vermont, U.S., Vital Records, 1720-1908

1880 census

1888 Find a Grave

Portrait and Biographical Album of Champaign County, Illinois, 1888. Page 878-879

"A Simple Story of Life and Love on the Dakota Plains" by John Manning Stewart. 2006. Posted to Ancestry.

Eveline Soper (1830–1895)

Eveline was born on December 12, 1830, in Georgia, Vermont. She married William Galaway possibly in 1850, the 1850 census lists them as married and living in Sheboygan, Wisconsin. They remained in Sheboygan Falls and can be found on the 1860, 1870 and 1880 census. Their daughter Clara is only observed on the 1860 census at 5 months old. Etta Galloway is only observed in the 1880 census at 9 years old.

On May 22, 1866 William was awarded patent #54,886 for an improved clothes drier. There is an example of one in the Smithsonian Museum of American History.

Eveline died from heart disease on December 28, 1895 and William died on March 26, 1916. Both are buried in Sheboygan Falls Cemetery. There is a stained glass memorial to Eveline at the Faith United Methodist Church in Sheboygan Falls possibly as part of the new renovations undertaken in 1901.

Migration:

1830 Georgia, Vermont

1850 Sheboygan Falls, Wisconsin

1895 Sheboygan Falls, Wisconsin

Children:

Alembert Peter Galaway (1854–1911)
Martha Galaway (1855–1914)
Clara Galaway (1859–)
Nellie Galaway (1860–1910)
Martin O. Galaway (1862–1955)
Etta Galaway (1871–)

Sources:

1850 census

1860 census

1880 census

Portrait and Biographical Album of Champaign County, Illinois, 1888. Page 878-879

1895 Find a Grave

1895 Wisconsin, U.S., Death Records, 1959-2004

Google Patent Collection, Patent #54886, https://patentimages.storage.googleapis.com/c3/59/0c/6a5df1e36b2b1c/US54886.pdf retrieved 21 August 2022.

Smithsonian Collection Museum of Natural History - Galaway Clothes Drier, https://collections.si.edu/search/detail/edanmdm:nmah_318218 retrieved 21 August 2022.

History of Faith United Methodist Church. https://www.faithumcshebfalls.org/church_history_909697 retrieved 11 December 2022.

Rachel Soper (1833–1899)

Rachel Soper was born on March 20, 1833, in Georgia, Vermont. In the 1850 census Rachel is living with her sister, Julia and her family in Sheboygan Falls, Wisconsin. Also listed in that census as a laborer is Orange Buck who was also born in Vermont. Rachel later married Orange Buck (1827-1910) in 1852 in Lake County, Illinois.

As seen in the 1860 census they eventually returned to Cambridge, Vermont after getting married in Illinois. The 1870 and the 1880 census has Rachel and Buck living in Johnson, Vermont where Rachel passed away on August 12, 1899, from chronic nephritis. Orange died in Essex, Vermont in 1910 and is buried in Greenwood Cemetery along with Rachel.

Migration:
1833 Georgia, Vermont
1850 Sheboygan Falls, Wisconsin
1860 Cambridge, Vermont
1870 Johnson, Vermont
1899 Johnson, Vermont

Children:
Chloe Hawley Buck (1858–1917)
Julia Buck (1861–1865)
Abijah Orange Buck (1869–1932)
Julia Sarah Buck (1869–1936)

Sources:
1850 census
1852 Marriage Record
1860 census
1870 census
1880 census
Portrait and Biographical Album of Champaign County, Illinois, 1888. Page 878-879
1899 Vermont, U.S., Vital Records, 1720-1908
1899 Find a Grave
1910 The Barre Daily Times. Barre, Vermont. 25 Oct 1910, Tue. Page 1.

Milton Hubble Soper (1836–1909)

Milton was born in Georgia, Vermont in April 1836. He came west to Lake County, Illinois in 1847 with his family and can be seen in the 1850 census living in Benton Township, Illinois. According to the Portrait and Biographical Album of Champaign County, Illinois, starting in 1852 he studied at the Waukegan Academy and eventually went to Lawrence University in Appleton Wisconsin for two years before finishing at the University of Michigan.

Milton returned home to marry his first cousin once removed, Catherine Soper (1845-1893) on January 18, 1862 in Waukegan, Illinois. Catherine is the daughter of Elijah Soper (1807-1887), who is the son of Remember Elijah's brother, Erastus Soper (1785-1857). In 1863 Milton bought a 360 acre farm in Franklin County, Vermont with his father before deciding to return to Harwood Township, Illinois in 1867. During this time, Milton and his brother, Orange Phelps Soper (1828-1888) engaged in some land speculation in southwest Missouri and Harwood Township, Illinois on land purchased from the Illinois Central Railroad Company. In 1868 Milton set roots in Harwood Township with his family where he established a prominent farm.

Catherine passed away in 1893 and is buried in Rantoul, Illinois. Milton remarried in 1895 to Frances Anderton Shepherd (1849–1923) and by 1900 he was living in Russell, Kansas. He passed away in Faribault, Minnesota on December 22, 1909, and was buried in Rantoul, Illinois at Elmwood Cemetery with his wife Catherine. His second wife Frances passed away in 1923 in Sioux City, Iowa and was also buried in Rantoul, Illinois at Elmwood Cemetery.

Migration:
1836 Georgia, Vermont
1847 Lake County, Illinois
1863 Vermont
1867 Harwood Township, Illinois
1900 Russell, Kansas
1905 Fairbault, MInnesota
1909 Fairbault, MInnesota

Children:
Cora May Soper (1865–1940)
Adrian Soper (1868–1941)
Arthur Milton Soper (1872–1953)
Stanley Livingstone Soper (1875–1960)
Morton Nay Soper (1878–1969)
Laura Edith Soper (1881–1971)

Sources:
1850 census
1852 Marriage Record
1860 census
1870 census
1880 census
Portrait and Biographical Album of Champaign County, Illinois, 1888. Page 878-879
1899 Vermont, U.S., Vital Records, 1720-1908
1899 Find a Grave

Phebe Soper (1796-1867)

Phebe Soper (1796-1867) was born in Milton, Vermont on March 27, 1896. She was the youngest of Mordecai and Naomi's children. She married John Bean (1781-1872) who was from New Hampshire. John Bean was previously married to Lois Tomlin (1783-1813) who died in 1813 in Milton, Vermont. Phebe is living in Milton with John in the 1850 and 1860 census.

Phebe died in Milton on February 11, 1867 and John in Milton on May 29, 1872 they are both buried in Miltonboro Cemetery.

Migration:
1796 Milton, Vermont
1867 Milton, Vermont

Children:
John Bean with Lois Tomlin
Elizabeth "Betsy" Bean (1805–1857)
Emily Bean (1808–)
Henry "Harry" Bean (1811–1890)
William Bean (1813–1895)
John Bean with Phebe Soper
Levi Sanderson Bean (1816–1900)
Joseph Bean (1819–1898)
Lois Cornelia Bean (1822–1901)
Sarah Maria Bean (1824–1916)

David R. Bean (1827–1891)
Emily Fidelia Bean (1830–1895)
John Bean (1837–1899)
Lucius Bean (1839–1839)

Sources:

1792 Vermont, U.S., Vital Records, 1720-1908 - Town of Milton Birth Record

1820 Census

1840 Census

1850 Census

1860 Census

1867 Vermont, U.S., Vital Records, 1720-1908 - Town of Milton Death Record

1867 Find A Grave

Gazetteer and business directory of Chittenden County, Vermont, for 1882-83.

Syracuse, N.Y., Printed at the Journal Office. 1882

History of Chittenden County, Vermont. Syracuse, N.Y. : D. Mason & Co.1886.

Levi Sanderson Bean (1816–1900)

Levi was born in Milton, Vermont on December 4, 1816. He married Cornelia Esther Hill (1824-1880) some time before 1847. The 1850 census shows them in Milton, Vermont. By the 1860 census they were located in Burke, New York. The 1870 census, the 1875 New York census, and the 1880 census also have them listed in Burke, New York. Cornelia died some time around 1880 in Burke and is buried in Constable Cemetery. Levi returned to Milton some time before the 1900 census where he passed away on August 27, 1900. His remains were returned to Burke where he was also buried at Constable Cemetery.

Migration:

1816 Milton, Vermont

1860 Burke, New York

1900 Milton,Vermont

Children:

Mary Bean (1847–1927)

Lewis Bean (1848–)

David Bean (1850–1919)

Ellen Bean (1853–1927)

Phebe Bean (1856–1873)

Emily Bean (1857–)

Olive Bean (1860–1878)

Sarah Bean (1862–1911)

John Bean (1865–1931)

Sources:

1850 census

1860 census

1870 census

1875 New York census

1880 census

1900 census

1900 Vermont, U.S., Vital Records, 1720-1908 - Town of Milton Death Record

1900 Find a Grave

Death notice - The Malone Palladium. September 06, 1900, Page 6. https://nyshistoricnewspapers.org/lccn/sn83031566/1900-09-06/ed-1/seq-6/print/image_681x461_from_2340%2C4312_to_3845%2C5331/

1927 Vermont, U.S., Vital Records, 1720-1908 - Town of Milton Death Record (Ellen Bean)

Joseph Bean (1819–1898)

Joseph was born in Milton, Vermont in 1819. Joseph married Henrietta Leonard (1825-1907). They lived in Milton together for their entire marriage. The 1850, 1860, 1870 census shows them living in Milton with Joseph's parents and his occupation is listed as a farmer, possibly he was helping his parents run the family farm. In the 1880 census his sister in-law Hortense Bean and his niece Hortense Bean were living with them in Milton. Hortense was married to Joseph's brother, John Bean (1837-1899) who was in Michigan working as a lumberman at the time.

There are listings on Find a Grave for two children, Lucius Bean 1839 and "Infant Daughter Bean 1849", who died in infancy that may be the children of Joseph and Henrietta. There is a death record for Lucius that indicates he passed away at two months, however there are no parents listed on the record. No additional records for "Infant Daughter Bean" have been located.

Joseph died in Milton on September 2,1898 and Henrietta died in Georgia, Vermont on March 6 1907. They are both buried in Miltonboro cemetery.

Migration:
1819 Milton, Vermont
1898 Milton, Vermont

Sources:
1839 Vermont, U.S., Vital Records, 1720-1908 - Town of Milton Death Record
1850 census
1860 census
1870 census
1880 census
History of Chittenden County, Vermont. Syracuse, N.Y. : D. Mason & Co.1886.

1898 Vermont, U.S., Vital Records, 1720-1908 - Town of Milton Death Record

1898 Find a Grave

1907 Vermont, U.S., Vital Records, 1720-1908 - Georgia Death Record (Henrietta)

Lois Cornelia Bean (1822–1901)

Lois was born in Milton, Vermont on January 31, 1822. She married Bernice Hill (1814-1896) some time in between the 1860 and 1870 census. The 1860 census shows her occupation as a servant and she is living with her sister, Emily Fidelia Bean (1830–1895) and her brother in law, Jonathan Blake (1828-1890) in Milton. By the 1870 census she was married to Bernice Hill and living in Georgia, Vermont with him and his daughter Jane Hill (1850-1912) from his first marriage to Sarah Ann Dunton (1823-1860) who died from typhoid fever/tuberculosis in 1860.

Bernice died in 1896 from stomach cancer and is buried in Miltonboro Cemetery. In the 1900 census Lois was living in Milton with her sister in law, Henrietta Bean, who was also widowed. Henrietta's husband Joseph Bean (1819-1898) died in 1898. Lois died on March 6, 1901, and is buried in Miltonboro Cemetery.

Migration:

1822 Milton, Vermont

1870 Georgia, Vermont

1900 Milton, Vermont

1901 Milton, Vermont

Children:

Bernice Hill (1814-1896) with Sarah Ann Dunton (1823-1860)

Jane Hill (1850-1912)

Bernice Hill (1814-1896) with Lois

None

Sources:
1860 census
1870 census
1880 census
1900 census
1901 Find a Grave
1901 Vermont, U.S., Wills and Probate Records, 1749-1999

Sarah Maria Bean (1824–1916)

Sarah was born on September 11, 1824 in Milton, Vermont. She married Charles Proctor Sanderson (1824-1911) on June 29, 1851 in Milton, Vermont. In the 1850 census she is living with her future in-laws in Milton, Vermont. She and Charles are found living together on the 1860, 1870, 1880, 1900, and 1910 census.

Charles died on April 7, 1911 in Milton Vermont. Sarah died on April 8, 1916 in Milton, Vermont. They are both buried in West Milton Cemetery.

Migration:
1824 Milton, Vermont
1916 Milton, Vermont

Children:
Willard Sanderson (1856–1936)
Charles L Sanderson (1858–1939)

Sources:
1850 census
1851 Vermont, U.S., Vital Records, 1720-1908 - Town of Milton Marriage Record
1860 census
1870 census]

1880 census

Gazetteer and business directory of Chittenden County, Vermont, for 1882-83.

Syracuse, N.Y., Printed at the Journal Office. 1882

1900 census

1910 census

1916 Find a Grave

1916 Vermont, U.S., Wills and Probate Records, 1749-1999

1939 Vermont, U.S., Death Records, 1909-2008 Town of Milton Death Record (Charles L Sanderson)

David Bean (1827–1891)

David was born on January 26, 1827 in Milton, Vermont. In the 1860 census he was living in Waukau, Wisconsin. By 1870 he was still living in Waukau, married to Julia Boardman (1835-1916) with two children. They are still living in Waukau in the 1880 census. Julia's maiden name, Boardman, was listed on their daughter Helen's marriage record from 1893.

David died on March 26, 1891 and is buried in Omro Cemetery. Julia died on March 7, 1916 and is also buried in Omro Cemetery.

Migration:

1827 Milton, Vermont

1860 Wakau, Wisconsin

Children:

Clarencc Bean (1864–1891)

Helen Margaret Bean (1869–1951)

Sources:

1860 census

1863 U.S., Civil War Draft Registrations Records, 1863-1865

1870 census

1880 census

1891 Find a Grave

1891 Wisconsin, U.S., Death Index, 1808-1907

1893 Wisconsin, U.S., Marriage Records, 1820-2004 for Helen Margart Bean (Julia Boardman)

Julia Bean Obituary The Oshkosh Northwestern. Oshkosh, Wisconsin. March 09, 1916. Page 5.

Emily Fidelia Bean (1830–1895)

Emily was born in MIlton, Vermont on April 30, 1830. She married Jonathan Blake on June 28, 1851 in Milton Vermont. They had one son together, William Blake (1853-1915). Emily and Jonanthan are living in Milton on the 1860, 1870, and 1880 census.

Jonathan died on August 12, 1890 and is buried in Miltonboro Cemetery. Emily died on May 12, 1895 and is also buried in Miltonboro Cemetery.

Migration:

1830 Milton, Vermont

1895 Milton, Vermont

Children:

William C Blake (1853–1915)

Sources:

1851 Vermont, U.S., Vital Records, 1720-1908 Town of Milton Marriage Record

1860 census

1870 census

1873 Vermont, U.S., Vital Records, 1720-1908 Town of Milton Marriage Record (William marriage record

1880 census

1895 Vermont, U.S., Vital Records, 1720-1908 Town of Milton Death Record

1895 Find a Grave

1895 Vermont, U.S., Wills and Probate Records, 1749-1999

1915 Vermont, U.S., Death Records, 1909-2008 (William death record)

John Bean (1837–1899)

John was born in Milton, Vermont on January 1, 1837. The 1850 census shows him living in Milton, Vermont with his parents. He registered for the draft in Pentwater, Michigan in mid-1863 where his marriage status is listed as single. John married Hortense Messmore (1842-1930) before the 1870 census which has them listed in Pentwater, Michigan with their son, John H. Bean (1867-1935), aged 2. John H Bean would later go on to attend the University of Vermont Medical College and become a doctor.

John's wife, Hortense would later remarry on April 4, 1886 to Edwin Miner (1838-?). There are no records that have been identified but the inference is that John and Hortense had separated prior to 1886.

One of the more interesting occupations listed for John is found in the Duluth (Minnesota) City Directory (1890-1892), where he is listed simply as an explorer. He has been alternately listed as a logger and a carpenter in other sources.

According to a Town of Milton death record John and Hortense's daughter, Hortense (1871-1891) died of insanity at the age of 20 on January 6, 1891. John passed away after battling heart failure on September 10, 1899. His son, John H. Bean had traveled West to tend to him in his final weeks. He returned with his father's body where he was buried in Miltonboro Cemetery. His former wife, Hortense was widowed by the 1900 census and she died on April 28, 1930 where she is buried in the Bean family plot in Miltonboro Cemetery.

Migration:
1837 Milton, Vermont
1870 Pentwater, Michigan
1899 Duluth, Minnesota

Children:
John H Bean (1867–1935)
Hortense Bean (1871–1891)

Sources:
1850 census
1863 U.S., Civil War Draft Registrations Records, 1863-1865, Pentwater, Michigan
1870 census
1880 census
1886 Vermont, U.S., Vital Records, 1720-1908 Town of Milton Marriage Record (Hortense Bean to Edwin Miner)
Duluth, Minnesota Directories, 1890-1892
1891 Vermont, U.S., Vital Records, 1720-1908 Town of Milton Death Record (Hortense)
1899 Minnesota, U.S., St. Louis County, Death Index, 1870-1899
1899 Find a Grave
Death Notice - The St. Albans Daily Messenger. 19 Sep 1899. Page 3.
Death Notice - The Earth. 23 Sep 1899. Page 4.
Death Notice - The Burlington Free Press. 25 Sep 1899. Page 7.
Death Notice - News and Citizen. 27 Sep 1899. Page 5.
Wedding Notice - The St. Albans Daily Messenger. Saint Albans, Vermont. October 17, 1899. Page 5.
1899 Vermont, U.S., Vital Records, 1720-1908 Marriage Record (John H. Bean)
1935 Vermont, U.S., Death Records, 1909-2008 Death Record (John H. Bean)

About The Author

Mr. Laycock lives in Maryland with his wife, three kids, four cats and one dog. He is a member of and serves on the board of managers of the Westminster Chapter of the Sons of the American Revolution. He has a deep interest in family genealogy and loves to uncover new stories and connections about his ancestors. In his free time he can be found watching the Chicago Cubs and still can't believe they finally won it all.

9 798218 169275